DIVINE ORDER OF ALCHEMY

The Ancient Secret to Union with God

The Divine Order of Alchemy: The Ancient Secret to Divine Union with God

Published by Villa Press

For further information, please contact:

Villa Press
P.O. Box 268
Eagle, ID 83616

Website Address: www.VillaPress.com (U.S. Inquiries) or
Website Address: www.ProdigalJourneys.com.

E-mail Address: contact@prodigaljourneys.com

Book Cover Design by: Teodora Chinde
www.nu-images.com

Editor/Producer:
Angela Clark
www.villapress.com

Printed in the United States
The Divine Order of Alchemy: The Ancient Secret to Divine Union with God
Daniel Clark
1. RELIGION/Christianity
2. BODY, MIND & SPIRIT/Spirituality

Library of Congress Control Number: 2015904097

ISBN 978-0-9794637-8-5 ISBN2 0-9794637-8-5

ACKNOWLEDGEMENTS

I'd like to thank Lisa James Vera for her countless revisions and amazing writing talent – truly incredible. You are so extremely gifted and we are grateful to have you on our team! Thank you! I'd also like to thank our talented artist – Teodora Chinde from Romania for the truly inspiring cover creation and loving patience as we found just the right cover for this book. Thank you! I'd like to thank Helen Crowley for all of her selfless support and valuable insights with the last two works. You are a treasure! Thank you! Lastly, I'd like to thank my wife Angela for all of her hard work and tireless hours editing, emailing, and endless revising of this book. You are my greatest inspiration! I love you from the bottom of my heart!

THE DIVINE ORDER OF ALCHEMY

The Ancient Secret to Union with God

By: Daniel Clark

Table of Contents

PREFACE

THE MIRACLE WORKINGS OF THE ALCHEMICAL ELECT

Have you ever said to yourself, "Where is the magic in my life? I read my Bible, I've read many self-help books, spiritual literature; I pray every day, I watch great inspirational movies and am inspired, but soon after, I find that the 'high' has worn off. I'm not changed, my situation is not changed. I wake up to the same reality as the day before."

Who are the alchemists of yesterday and today? The alchemists were people, men and women, who chose to step out of mediocrity and into magnificence. The alchemists choose to dig deep into the mysterious life to find the golden nuggets of life's transforming truths.

When these divine nuggets of truth are discovered, the life of the discoverer is changed forever. Alchemy begins materializing in all aspects of his life. His spiritual connection is forever solidified. The chains are off; he finally has the power to create for himself and his family as he wills. He deciphers truth from falsehood; his sight is finally open to the many mysteries of life. He is now free to create as he chooses – with divine co-operation – a more prosperous life. He enjoys contentment and harmony with all people. His peace and joy are permanent fixtures within himself. Synchronicities abound at every turn and life becomes a very magical place for him.

If your soul is yearning for such a great purpose in life – this is not by accident. The great alchemist, Jesus, who walked on water, raised the dead, cured the sick, gave sight to the blind, turned water into wine, said in John 14:12 that not only will we do what He did, but even *greater* works than he did.

So here we have a great promise from the greatest alchemist – Jesus. This promise speaks to the alchemist in all of us. Are you willing to do these greater things that the Master promised? Have you said to yourself, "I want truth at all costs?"

Many times it's been said that divine truth can be a light so bright that it can collapse a person's whole infrastructure of knowingness.

If you feel ready for this kind of truth, the truth that sets you free, then I would love to share with you the secrets that have been revealed to me, the ancient secret to divine union, where ALL things are possible.

I'm going to take you to the Holy Place – The Tabernacle in the Wilderness as mentioned in the Old Testament of the Bible – and it is here that we will not only ***view*** this Holy Tabernacle in the Wilderness, but must also begin digging through to the allegories/myths of this temple to find the underlying gold nuggets of pure truth. It is here that we will find the transformational properties of this Holy Place.

As these new truths begin to pierce the veil of your understanding, just allow it to happen. You may actually feel like you've finally come home to the truth, or you could feel a variety of other emotions. So cry if you need to. Get angry, feel the fear, but don't stop. Whatever the case, remember that when new information comes into our consciousness, many times we want to reject it immediately and say it isn't so. That is because of our made-up minds, the same mind that has had you in a prison (matrix) of mediocrity up until now. So if you're ready, let's let go and let God reveal some of his greater truths.

THE DIVINE ORDER OF ALCHEMY

INTRODUCTION

Ever since mankind, the prodigal spirit sons of our Father in Heaven, wandered into the wilderness of the world and fed upon the husks of its pleasures, which starve the body, there has been within man's heart a soundless voice urging him to return; but most men are so engrossed in material interests that they hear it not. [Anyone] who has heard this inner voice feels impelled by an inner urge to seek for the Lost Word; to build a house of God, a temple of the spirit, where he may meet the Father face to face and answer His call.

~ Max Heindel, *Ancient and Modern Initiation,* 1986

Imagine that you just got an invitation in the mail (or in today's electronic age, more likely via email) that reads something like this:

You're Invited!

WHO: You

WHAT: Union with God

WHEN: Right Now

What would you do? Would you have a ready RSVP at hand?

You may think I'm being tongue-in-cheek. I'm not. This invitation is being extended to you, right now, and I'm not making a joke. It's real. More than a book, this volume you've picked up and started reading today is an invitation. You are honestly invited to become one with God. You are invited to meet God – not figuratively, but face-to-face.

Since you have picked up this book I have to wonder if perhaps you have reached the end of yourself. You've fought long and hard, and you're exhausted. You're beaten. You no longer have the capacity to deal with or make sense of the chaos, mayhem, rat-race, rut, mediocrity, or downright morass of worldly life. As Heindel said in the opening quote, you have "wandered into the wilderness of the world and fed on the husks of its pleasures, which starve the body" (Heindel, 1986). Take heart: coming to the end of yourself only means you are primed and ready to make the journey toward grace. You're ready to surrender.

The current status of your mind is based on where you are and what you have experienced. Who are the people who have taught and influenced you? Did you have healthy parents and teachers or unhealthy ones? What information has been impressed on you until it's become embedded in your subconscious? What are the limits – lies, addiction, dysfunction, abusive relationships, unfulfilling jobs, religious dogma – that you have allowed to dictate your existence? What stories do you tell, what excuses do you make for sticking inside those limits? Now you must leave the excuses behind. Like Wayne Dyer says, "Excuses begone!" (Dyer, 2011). And I am telling you unequivocally that the only way to move beyond the excuses and access the part of yourself – your "self" – that needs to break those limiting shackles and emerge into freedom and wholeness is through co-operation with God.

Divine Alchemy

This book outlines a pathway toward meeting God face-to-face through a process called divine alchemy. Defined simply, *alchemy* means taking something common and transforming it into something of great value (Merriam-Webster, Inc., 2014). "Alchemy AL or EL means God or shining. KHEM or CHEM is from the root (Greek) KIMIA which means to fuse. Therefore, Alchemy means to fuse with God or the Shining-To Be Enlightened (Gnosis: The Secret of Solomon's Temple Revealed. Philip Gardiner 2006) Many authors have characterized alchemy as a Middle Age science which was the precursor to modern chemistry. This is a misconception; alchemy in fact represented a secret base of knowledge founded on the premise that Nature taken as a whole was a living, evolving, and holy being (Robertson, 2009). Middle Age alchemists believed, for example, that metals were growing, evolving organisms and envisioned mining ore as a sort of birthing process (Robertson, 2009). Much more important, though, is the underlying connection identifying the alchemical quest as a spiritual journey that symbolizes the regeneration of the human soul (Debus, 2004). In modern times spiritual teacher Natalie Reid has described alchemy as "a path and a practice that allow us to listen to the voice of our own soul" (Reid, 2008). Thus in the present context I use the term to describe a pathway toward meeting God and becoming one with Him.

Divine alchemy is a moving beyond the popular phenomenon that many Christians call, "finding Jesus", and alchemy which is birthing *the* Christos within us. During the course of this book you will come to understand the difference between the two and recognize why we will want to understand the further esoteric meaning behind Jesus, the Christ which is alchemy (Union with God). Divine alchemy means taking something common (the perceived duality between your "self" and "God") and turning it into something infinitely and gloriously magnificent (merging and co-operating with God for the first time).

Several Scriptural passages refer to such union, to relinquishing the notion that there are two separate entities "me" and "God" and becoming one with the Father: "They will ask the way to Zion, with their faces toward it, saying, 'Come and let us **join ourselves to the Lord** in a perpetual covenant that will not be forgotten'" (Ezekiel 50:5). "[those] Who **join themselves to the Lord**, to serve Him, And to love the name of the Lord, to be His servants… Even them I will bring to My holy mountain, And make them joyful in My house of prayer" (Isaiah 56:6-7). "Then join them one to another for yourself into one stick, and **they will become one** in your hand" (Ezekiel 37:17). "For [Christ] himself is our peace, who **has made the two one** and has destroyed the barrier, the dividing wall of hostility, by abolishing in his flesh the law…His purpose was to create in himself **one new man out of the two**, thus making peace, and in this **one body to reconcile both of them to God** through the cross…" (Ephesians 2:14-15, emphasis mine). "…that all of them may be one, Father, just as you are in me and I am in you. May they also be in us so that the world may believe that you sent me" (John 17:21 NIV). If we believe Scripture, how can we reject the truth and attainability of divine union?

You can meet God face-to-face. You can see with God's eyes. You can traverse the pathway of alchemy and walk with God, all day and every day. You and God can become one.

Alchemy is the way to enlightenment—to ultimate union with God. And there is even greater promise in that union than enlightenment. Following this path offers you the key to prosperity, to "have life, and have it more abundantly" (John 10:10). The end result of divine alchemy is to unlock for you the riches of God's Kingdom. You shall "spend your days in prosperity. And your years in pleasures"

(Job 36:11); you "shall dwell in prosperity. And your descendants shall inherit the earth" (Psalm 25:13). In the pages that follow you will learn how to surrender your excuses, break free of the matrix that encases your mind, and walk the path of alchemy to meet God face-to-face; and if you do so you will gather the fruits of the Kingdom in your earthly life. I mean this literally. You will have life, and you will have it more abundantly (according to Jesus). As in money in your pocket. As in rewarding work that pays well. As in freedom from addiction and abuse. As in love, hope, and fulfillment – whatever it is that you need. "For your Father knows the things you have need of before you ask Him" (Matthew 6:8).

The alchemist's path is not easy; it is arduous and treacherous ("the road leading to life is narrow and cramped and few are finding it" Matthew 7:14). The limits surrounding your mind will fight you all the way. The matrix of lifelong human limited understanding is the prison bonds that the Holy Spirit must break to set us free. And there is a progression that will be discussed in this book. Much like battling addiction according to a Twelve Step Program, you probably will find yourself backsliding from time to time. But when you step back onto the path you'll find that all is not lost – you get to start up again right where you left off.

To make the pathway a little easier, I find mental imagery to be helpful. That's why I have organized this book according to a metaphor. This symbolism, found in the Old Testament, will help you create mental pictures on which you can meditate and that will illuminate and guide your steps along the initiate's path. The metaphor I have chosen is the Tabernacle in the Wilderness.

The Tabernacle in the Wilderness

When Moses led the Israelites out of Egypt, they wandered for years in the wilderness before reaching the Promised Land. Because they were constantly on the move they had no permanent structure within which to worship. So God instructed Moses to have the Israelites build a portable temple, sort of a tent they could carry along on their travels. "Let them make Me a sanctuary, that I may dwell among them" (Exodus 25:8). This structure became the Tabernacle in the Wilderness.

God was very specific in His instructions about how the Tabernacle should be built. He laid out the exact proportions, the materials, the construction, and the decorations in meticulous detail. Poles of acacia wood overlaid with gold…a seven-branched Lampstand of pure hammered gold…ten linen curtains dyed blue, purple, and scarlet and woven with images of cherubim…Read Exodus 25-40 and you'll see just how lengthy and precise those directions were. But memorizing the exact cubit dimensions of the Tabernacle and how many flowers were to be carven on the Lampstand is not what's important here. Like much of the Old Testament, the description of the Tabernacle is pure allegory. Each chamber of the Tabernacle serves as a philosophical symbol of a greater truth. Those who hear the call of the Holy Spirit within are invited to enter the "gate," walk through each "chamber," and stop at each "station" one by one – in order – and thus be made ready finally to enter the Temple, the Holy of Holies, and meet God face-to-face.

The symbolic meanings surrounding the Tabernacle in the Wilderness are treated with great love and eloquence in the book *Ancient and Modern Initiation* by Max Heindel (1865-1919), a Seer of The Rosicrucian Fellowship (Heindel, 1986). Heindel explains that the Tabernacle "…was the embodiment of great cosmic truths hidden by a veil of symbolism which spoke to the inner or Higher Self." As the Tabernacle was God's dwelling among men, likewise your body is the dwelling place of God's divine Nature which cannot be separated from your soul. The tabernacle we will be discussing will be reconstructed inside your own body and mind.

Here is a pictorial diagram of the literal Tabernacle:

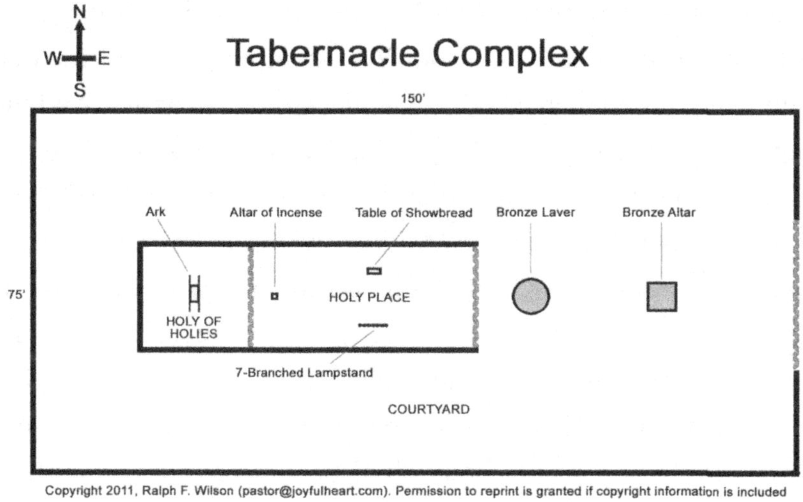

Note: This literal tabernacle (temple) is also the Spiritual temple that God will rebuild in us. The temple thus becomes *portable* because it is something that we take with us wherever we go.

So the steps along the alchemical pathway will be a series of mystical steps through the tabernacle in the wilderness. We are going to discover the hidden ancient secrets to this walk through the tabernacle which are as follows:

1. Surrender your "self" by laying yourself on the bronze altar and give yourself up to God; and enter the gate.
2. Bathe in the bronze laver
3. Walk into the holy place
4. Take communion at the table of showbread
5. Light the candles on the Lampstand
6. Enter the Holy of Holies

7. Witness the Ark of the Covenant
8. Meet God face-to-face
9. Experience Union with God

Again, it is not the absolute physical or corporeal application of the metaphor that is important. What's important is going through the process of getting ready to meet God. You must be prepared for that sacred union with the Father. That's what alchemy is all about. And the initial step is surrendering the idea of duality. You must give up the notion of the solitary "I" as unique and separate from God and from the Holy Spirit. There's a verse in Matthew which is translated in the New King James Bible as "The lamp of the body is the eye. If therefore your eye is good, your whole body will be full of light" (Matthew 6:22). However, I prefer the earlier King James Bible translation which reads, "The light of the body is the eye. If therefore thine eye be **single**, thy whole body shall be full of light" (Matthew 6:22, Authorized King James Version, 1611, 1769, emphasis mine). That is, if your eye (your "I") becomes single (read: unified with God) your whole body will be filled with God's light. You will be made of light and you will shine the light of the Father into the world.

"For now we see in a mirror, dimly, but then **face to face**. Now I know in part, but then **I shall know just as I also am known**" (1 Corinthians 13:7-13; emphasis mine). You are tired of walking down the crazy road you're on, you've had enough. The prodigal son is ready to come home. You are finished with your ideologies and negative thoughts and addictions and limitations. You are ready to move into a grander sense of self. And the reason why I say "grander" is because we are made in God's image and likeness. We are a facet of the divine. We are infinite beings. We are the Father's and He is us (our very breath). The Father wants to shine through us magnificently, in a unique way through each of us. Surrender is the key to the

Kingdom within; it is the Tabernacle gateway. By surrender we can move further down the alchemical path toward the temple of grace, the Holy of Holies.

You are invited into union with God. Let this be your RSVP: Take the first step, surrender and enter the Tabernacle in the Wilderness.

CHAPTER 1:

DIVINE ALCHEMY VERSUS THE SPELL OF MEDIOCRITY, or WHAT THIS BOOK IS ABOUT

The boy gathers materials for a temple, and then when he is thirty, concludes to build a woodshed.
~ Henry David Thoreau

It is mediocrity which makes laws and sets mantraps and spring-guns in the realm of free song, saying thus far shalt thou go and no further.
~ James Russell Lowell

Now that you're just getting started, this is a good time to ask: Dan, why did you write this book? What is its purpose? Why has it come into my hands at this particular moment? How does it differ from any other Christian (or Buddhist, or Hindu, or Kabalistic, or whatever) how-to manual that ostensibly will teach me how to pray, meditate, find Jesus, be saved, get into Heaven, or strike up a relationship with God?

Those are good questions. And I have an equally good answer, which starts by telling you not what this book is, but what it isn't: it is not about finding Jesus. It is not about getting saved and reserving a space up in Heaven (which, by the way, you can only enjoy after you die). It's not about compartmentalization, delusion, or limitation. It's not about religiosity or settling for the restricted, constricted benefits our earthly religions have to offer. It's not about mediocrity.

So what is it about? It's about real transformation. It's about turning base metal into gold. The Tabernacle in the Wilderness is a metaphor for the pathway that leads to divine alchemy. And divine alchemy is a metaphor for transforming your lower nature into pure spirit.

Yesterday I was talking with a Christian gentleman who reminded me so much of my own mindset during my 40-year stint as a Jehovah's Witness. Apparently this guy's mantra was "I'm a sinner," because he kept saying it over and over. He would say, "I believe in Jesus," but inevitably follow up with, "I'm a sinner." "Okay," I thought, "You're a sinner. But is that not your choice?"

His religiosity had compartmentalized him. What I mean is that by self-identifying as an eternal sinner he was sticking himself in a compartment and calling it destiny. He had gotten saved at the altar and become a Christian so he could say, "I'm a Christian. I believe in Jesus." But simultaneously he was giving himself *carte blanche* to continue living down in the flesh, living life from his ego, pursuing all his self-serving motives and making it okay by summoning up that grand excuse, "I'm a sinner." He probably thought he had the best of all worlds. That couldn't be farther from the truth.

Here's the character of his delusion: his flesh was ruling even while his voice said, "I'm a Christian." He didn't realize that splitting oneself that way, where one half lives in the flesh and the other half says, "I believe," strips all the power out of the equation. Christianity puts a spell on its followers – a spell of mediocrity; a spell of compartmentalization; a spell of limitation; of living in partial truth and being okay with that. But there's no power in limits. There's no transformation in sticking oneself in a box and slapping on a label. People answer the altar call and get "saved," but they don't transform. They don't make any real change because they don't want to give up all the desires of the ego – desires like addiction, disease, thinking their religion is the one and only path, hating and condemning everyone who doesn't follow their way. People settle for living out of their base natures, their lower natures, and religiosity makes it all okay.

The same thing happened in Jesus' time. The first Christians were limited too. They read by the letter of the law; they studied their Bibles and called each other brothers, they praised one another. Yet Jesus – Jesus the accused – He was the one going about performing miracle after miracle. He was the one out there raising the dead, healing the crippled, casting out demons, and feeding crowds. He was out doing the deeds while they rested on the formalities.

Now I don't mean to pick on Christianity. Christian churches are no worse or better than any other religion in this regard. I only use Christianity as an example because it's so much a part of Western society. The same thing happens to Buddhists, Hindus, Muslims, Jehovah's Witnesses, and Jews – it happens in any religion that directs you to look for some deity "out there." Christian churches send you to find Jesus "out there." In other religions it's God "out there," Allah "out there," Buddha "out there." They tell you to go into the church or temple or synagogue and worship your deity of choice. Like my Christian friend, who had been told he was okay just the way he was. He could go ahead and be a sinner; all he had to do was attend church and sing praises and that's as good as it gets.

The churches are wrong. Your lower nature, or what's been called the serpent energy (as in Satan or Lucifer), can be transcended. Greek mythology painted images of people with their heads on the serpent or the serpent wrapped around their waists. But at the same time they had one hand wrapped around the serpent's neck. Those images illustrate how the spirit dominates serpent energy. By tapping into the pure spirit the Christian with the "I'm a sinner" mantra could have transcended his "sin" and unleashed an indescribable power in its place. You can bring that serpent under control, and this book will show you how.

But that's not all. This book is about real alchemy, true transformation. Not denial, delusion, accepting the limitations and spouting out powerless "I believes." We are going to break the spell of mediocrity that religiosity is selling.

In Biblical times Jesus offered his followers the same abilities He had: "He who believes in Me, the works that I do he will do also, and **greater works than these** he will do" (John 14:12; emphasis mine). Jesus didn't want to be worshipped. He didn't just want people to sit in a church and sing His praises. Rather, He wanted to show the world that this power, the power of Spirit, lives in all of us and will be raised up within us – for us to use – if we only ask. That's what He meant when He said "Ask, and it will be given to you; seek, and you will find; knock, and it will be opened to you" (Matthew 7:7). Rather than looking for Jesus "out there," the Christ (the anointing) is going to be given birth to and raised up *in you.* It lives inside you even now. So "I believe in Jesus," is not the end of the story. That's demonstration. *Transformation*, in contrast, happens when you stop settling and instead you yourself fully embrace the Christos (the anointing that is lying dormant within us). This Christhood is raised up within you until eventually there is less and less of self, the ego, and God – the Christos becomes more and more within us until finally mediocrity, hopelessness, desperation, illness and poverty come to naught.

That's what this book is about: the pathway out of mediocrity.

You will learn to identify and free yourself from the delusional compartment into which you've been placed. You will transcend serpent energy and unleash the perfect Christ within you. You will become like Jesus and see miracles in your own life.

It all starts with breaking out of the matrix, and that's what I want to talk about in the next chapter.

CHAPTER 2:

THE MATRIX

You have to let it all go, Neo. Fear, doubt, and disbelief. Free your mind.
~ Morpheus, *The Matrix,* 1999

The Wachowski Brothers' 1999 sci-fi film drama *The Matrix* depicts the explosive journey of a mild-mannered computer hacker to discovering that his mind is not his own. Rather, he's being controlled by a massive artificial intelligence system that's overtaken earth and harnessed humanity as its energy source. In its day *The Matrix* was a major blockbuster. Now why would a film about mind control be so popular? Perhaps it reflects humans' penchant for debating the true nature of reality. Developing a notion of what's real – and what isn't – is part of the human condition.

Adopting the film's definition of matrix (i.e. a computer-generated reality simulation), I'd like to suggest that every one of us has a mind-control matrix. We build matrices like little boxes around our minds and then live under the constrictions of those frameworks. They become the hardwiring in our mind-computers. Everything we think, feel, say, and do generates from within that box – our individual matrix sets the agenda. Our entire perception and world view is tinted the color of our box walls. And how are these boxes constructed? They're inherited in our DNA. They're passed along from generation to generation through family tradition and parental discipline. They're erected by church leaders and religious dogma. They're built from the compulsions created by addiction and codependency.

Our matrices are our belief systems. Any set of beliefs in which we're completely invested and to which we hand over absolute control becomes our matrix. That includes religion, family or cultural tradition, political ideology, abusive cycles, addiction and codependence. We build a mental structure according to the definition of reality set forth by that belief system, and then grant the structure ownership and control over our minds and actions.

Say you grew up in poverty. Eventually you become so accustomed to being broke that you start seeing through poor eyes. "That's just the way it is," you say. "This is who I am, I'm poor." And guess what? You stay broke. Poorness becomes your mantra, your belief system. It defines your identity. Can you see how believing being poor is "just the way it is" becomes a prophecy that fulfills itself? That point where you completely believe something is "just the way it is" is the moment when your matrix is constructed. It happens the same way with any belief: "I'm an alcoholic. That's the way it is. I can't help it. My mother was an alcoholic. Life's hard, but that's just the way it is." The walls go up and the matrix takes control. Have you ever known a woman who was being abused by a violent husband? From a safe position outside the relationship it's easy to say, "How can she stay in that marriage? Her husband beats her senseless every weekend!" Abuse is her personal matrix. She's embraced "that's just the way it is."

Religious values perhaps form the ultimate matrix. People go to church and sure, they feel good for a couple of hours. In God's house they sit with their neighbors and feel communion with God. But once they walk outside those four walls for so many folks that feeling of connection soon dissipates. They wonder where God is now. Then they lose their job or a beloved aunt dies, and they think, "That's it. There is no God; a good God wouldn't let such horrible things happen." Or they blame God for their troubles. Shame and blame, fear and doubt are the cornerstones of the matrix built around much of today's religious ideology.

Of course, not all belief systems are bad. Some religions are better than others; better, that is, in terms of actual empowerment. While some churches base their teachings on fear and shame, others do strive toward higher consciousness, enlightenment, and at-one-ment with God. There are healthful matrices and unhealthy ones; it's probably better to be addicted to exercise than to heroin. But whatever the character of our matrix, it becomes the eyes through which we see. Our matrices own us.

I'm here to tell you there's a better way: Union with God. And union with God brings freedom from the matrix. This book offers a set of directions for rewiring your hard drive. It describes the pathway out of your box. The directions are simple, but the path will not be easy. Undoing a belief system is very, very difficult. Breaking down the matrix walls requires first that you surrender to a power greater than yourself. It's no coincidence that surrender to a higher power is one of the Twelve Steps followed by Alcoholics Anonymous. Your belief system rules your mind. Like maybe an alcoholic decides on his own to quit drinking. Then a day later he's back on the bottle. Alcohol is his ruling entity; it's the all-knowing power residing in his mind. In order to break the alcohol/box/matrix that's controlling him, he has to form a union and become one with divinity – merge with the divine – surrender his "self" to a higher power to experience the grace that will override his programming.

In the introduction I explained that surrender is the first gate. It's the beginning step down the initiate's path to divine alchemy. My earlier book, *Surrender: Your Key to the Kingdom Within*, describes how surrender consists of an overshadowing. You must become willing to get out of your matrix, and then you must allow the Holy Spirit which is ultimate truth to overshadow your mind. You must surrender "my will" for the divine will and trade your matrix for oneness with God.

Lots of people want to get out of their matrices. You may ask how I know that, so let me tell you a story: the other day I was in a church. At the end of service the pastor did a slightly-modified altar call. He asked the whole congregation to close their eyes. Then he asked everyone who wanted to be connected with God, to know God for the first time, to stand up right there in their spots. When I opened my eyes, I was stunned to see that the majority of the congregation (500 people) was on their feet! I started to cry. "There cannot be this many people who don't know God. There can't be this many disconnected people." It blew me away. But then I realized right there that there limitation was that their inner temples were not being constructed properly. These Christians were obviously in denial. They were doing the same thing over and over habitually worshiping Jesus exteriorly, but refusing to realize that Christ dwells within them. So in continuing to do this, there is an obvious disconnect between them and God. Failure to look at the ills within us/separation with God shows that we're in a matrix of Christian religiosity. And my heart went out to all those poor people who wanted to break out of the boxes that rule their minds but had not yet found the way.

Here's another example. About a week after the altar call I was watching *The 700 Club*. They aired an interview with a Hungarian politician who had been a prominent member of an anti-Semitic political party. Csanád Szegedi had served as vice president of the highly anti-Semitic Jobbik Party (hater of Jews) for six years. Watching the video I was struck by his appearance as a party leader – all dressed in black like a Fascist. Yet *The 700 Club*'s reason for showing the Szegedi interview was because in 2013 his 94-year-old grandmother revealed astonishing news: Szegedi was, in fact, a Jew. Most of his family had been annihilated at Auschwitz. This news had a profound effect on Szegedi. First he was forced to leave the Jobbik Party. Although at first he resisted his Jewish roots, after a while he decided to visit a rabbi. He began taking classes in Judaism and learning Hebrew. Eventually he entirely embraced his heritage and became a full-on practicing, devout Jew.

Why is this story important to my book? To me, here's the important take-away message: one day Szegedi was a Fascist. His matrix was anti-Semitism. He was a leader in a large anti-Semitic political party. So then what happened when he found out he was a Jew? A rabbi took his hand and led him into the Jewish faith, into another indoctrination tank. All Szegedi did was trade one matrix for another. He was a Fascist because he believed he was a Fascist. Now he's a Jew, because he believes he's a Jew – another box to structure his identity. A better outcome would have been for Szegedi to learn instead that he's made in the image and likeness of God, that he's a divine idea in God's mind. That's the bigger reality into which we are all invited. That's freedom from the matrix.

You are being invited into a union with God. Union with God! Now that's a reality to blow your mind. And union with God is there within everyone's reach. We all are invited. When you make the choice to seek union with God and you surrender yourself by metaphorically laying yourself on the altar (which is the first chamber in the tabernacle), you have stepped onto the path of the initiate. It's a pathway you must traverse from start (laying yourself on the altar) to finish (face-to-face with God or Union). The path is difficult. Many obstacles lie along the way; and the first block is denial. Like Neo in *The Matrix*, we don't want to believe in any reality where our minds are not our own. We deny our matrices. Denial is the first blockage on the initiate's path, and the topic of the next chapter.

CHAPTER 3:

COMING OUT OF DENIAL

I sometimes wonder whether our churches—living as we do in American death-denying culture, smiling through our praise choruses—are inadvertently helping people live not as much in hope as in denial.
~ Mark Galli, Editor *Christianity Today*

As I've said, alchemy is an ancient concept describing the process of transmuting a common substance into something of great value. Divine alchemy, then, means taking your base and common "self" and transfusing it into a union with God, realizing that promise of oneness with God to which you have been invited. The prodigal son must make the journey home into the temple and enter into at-one-ment with the Father. The ring of union will be placed on his finger and he will be reestablished in God's light.

So the next step along the initiate's pathway is to allow an overshadowing. It's very similar to the first three steps in the Twelve Steps set forth by Alcoholics Anonymous:

1. We admitted we were powerless over alcohol—that our lives had become unmanageable.

2. Came to believe that a Power greater than ourselves could restore us to sanity.
3. Made a decision to turn our will and our lives over the care of God *as we understood him.*

In step 1, substitute for the word "alcohol" whatever constructs your own personal matrix: drugs, abuse, sexual addiction, fear-based religious ideology, having horrible money problems, whatever. The key to beginning your journey toward divine alchemy is to let go of "self"-control and become overshadowed by the Holy Spirit. But be aware that your "self" will resist. Your matrix does not want to relinquish control; it will set up roadblocks in your way. This blockage is called denial.

Psychologists and counselors understand denial as a mental defense mechanism. It's a method the brain uses to cope with the grief associated with the death of a loved one or another distressful situation. To avoid facing up to the shock and pain, we simply refuse to acknowledge the situation. The most common events people meet with denial are death, life-threatening health issues, the end of a relationship, and job loss. Now in the case of catastrophic loss a little denial may be a good thing; it gives your mind time to adjust to the painful truth. But serious problems arise when denial persists over time. Denial might prevent you from getting help or dealing with issues that then spiral out of control, with devastating long-term consequences. Along the path to divine alchemy, removing the roadblock of denial is crucial to starting the journey toward enlightenment, to Christhood, to union with the Father.

Let's go back to the example of the alcoholic. Isn't it interesting to hear on the news about a drunk driver who runs into and kills a group of nurses? And this man's life has hit rock bottom. His wife has left him; he's living at the Red Cross. He has nothing. But the first words out of his mouth are, "I'm not an alcoholic." We all look at this guy and think, "How can he say he's not an alcoholic? Look at him! He's lost everything. He's drinking himself to death." That's denial. And coming out of denial represents the very first of the Twelve Steps of Alcoholics Anonymous. Remember? "We admitted we were powerless…our lives had become unmanageable." This man refused to admit that the poison alcohol was making him sick and was the source of all his problems. That's denial.

It's no different with the victim of domestic abuse. Say your woman friend shows up at your house with two black eyes. Yet she's telling you, "I love my husband, and I know he loves me." You look at her bruises and think, "No he doesn't. He's narcissistic, he's crazy, and he's going to kill you if you don't get out of there." She's in denial. Her mind has erected obstacles that allow her to deny the reality she's living in. Why? Because admitting abuse would mean admitting her own vulnerability; it would mean giving up all sense of control.

Now consider religious ideology. On the surface of entering most churches, everything seems most wonderful. The brothers and sisters are happy to see one another. Worship time begins and everyone begins singing praises to Jesus. It's beautiful! The study begins and everyone opens their Bibles and follows the Pastor. But soon after, church is over. Everyone embraces one another and says, "Good-bye." Many times, my wife and I have been asked over to one or more of the brothers' or sisters' homes, only to find out that there is a severe disconnect between them and God. Some of them are still smoking heavily, a lot are over-drinking, many suffer from severe depression, and many think they are not growing in the Lord. So the question that I ask myself is that if this is how they really feel? Why would they continue to go to church to get these results over and over? I think this is another form of denial. I think we have to ask ourselves, "If I'm not growing in my relationship with God then don't I need to examine what it is that I'm doing?" Jesus said, "Don't marvel at these things, for these and greater you will do." So I think the normal question for all of us to ask is, "Why am I not doing the greater things?" I think many times we do things out of habit, which is our matrix. Einstein's definition of insanity is doing the same things over and over and expecting a different outcome (our matrix). It takes great humility to be able to look at our matrix and admit to ourselves that something's missing. To admit that we're not growing. To admit that we're unhappy. We're addicted. We're angry, frustrated, etc. All of us are being called out of our matrices by God himself and being called into divine union which transforms every aspect of our lives, including our religious perspectives.

Denial based on religious ideology not only blocks the path toward union with God, it blocks the way to enjoying the riches of the Kingdom too. Just the other day I spoke with a guy who had lost his home to foreclosure. I asked him what he was doing about it. "The Lord is my savior," he told me. "The Lord is my shepherd. I believe in Jesus." That was it! And the last time I touched base with this guy he had lost his home and still struggles monthly to pay his new rent; there's an eviction notice on his door almost every month; and yet he still doesn't want to do anything except believe in Jesus. That's the Christian form of denial. You can't just say, "I believe in Jesus," and expect magically to be made whole and complete. No matter how many times you say it. God wants our partnership. He wants us to come into union with Him, to meet us in the Holy of Holies. He wants his prodigal sons and daughters to come home and to walk in oneness with Him. Then we will see that prosperity in our lives. When God places that ring on our finger, the symbol of union with Him, we get to use that ring like a credit card. Prosperity, riches, wealth, love, fulfillment all will materialize in our lives as we need them. The eviction notices will come off our doors.

Contrast that Christian form of denial – repeating "I believe in Jesus" and nothing more – with true enlightenment. To me a person who's truly enlightened is solid, whole, and complete. He trusts. He has learned to rest in the Lord and walk through life with power rather than passivity. She knows how to create and work with others; she embraces others outside her own religiosity. He walks in oneness not just with God, but also with other people. The enlightened have merged with the spiritual dimension within so that they are illuminated from the inside. You can see that light shining out of them. They have important things to say and they want to speak. They contribute to society. They are powerful, never weak or feeble. The enlightened now are like Jesus – they're doing the greater things, opening the eyes of the blind. They can give dumb people tongues, or deaf people hearing and make the crippled leap like gazelles. They speak truth from the heart, from the illumined place.

This is the place to which you want to travel. But first you must come out of denial. And I mean your denial – no one else's – yours.

Many people want to reach that place. They want the magic, to lean on Moses' staff and to do the greater things. But they don't want to come out of denial. No; they'd rather keep on doing the same things over and over. I have a dear friend who lives in denial. He's a Jehovah's Witness; his life is hell and he's always the victim. But he keeps pushing back the notion that the false ideology of the churches Christian perspectives is running (and ruining) his life – pushing that thought way, way back into the far reaches of his mind and hoping things will get better. Things won't get any better. The alcoholic doesn't get better by denying he has an alcohol problem. The terminally ill cancer patient won't get better by pretending the cancer isn't there.

Release will come when you stand up to the illusion. Coming out of denial means facing up and saying, "I feel like crap. I'm not connected. I don't believe Christ is real. I don't believe there is a God because I can't feel him." Denial will end when we stand up to the illusionment, to the limitations, to the fear. Think of it like this: we are going to die one way or another. We can die in the illusion. Or we can die *to* the illusion and be reborn by the Holy Spirit.

Emerging from denial is the invitation for the Holy Spirit to come in and start working to dismantle our egos, our "selves." I call this a crucifixion. I'm often amused when I hear Christians talking as if Jesus was the only person who was ever crucified. If we are to be born into the spiritual realm and build cooperation between that spiritual realm and our realm, we must be born anew. And rebirth requires death. I'm not talking about the death of your corporeal body; I'm talking about the death of our illusions, our false self and many of our ideologies. The symbolism of the sacrifices on the altar (in the tabernacle) is that we have to surrender some of what we know – maybe all of what we know. Our temples have to be torn down and rebuilt by God. "Or do you not know that your body is the temple of the Holy Spirit who is in you, whom you have from God, and you are not your own?" (1 Corinthians 6:19). I ask people, "Where are your temples?" and they point to the sides of their heads. That makes me laugh because that's exactly where your temple is – inside your head.

When we surrender to the Holy Spirit we walk through the Tabernacle gate and lay ourselves down on the bronze altar for sanctification. We lay our lives down as a sacrifice to God (a metaphorical crucifixion). That's the allegorical meaning behind those Biblical instructions for constructing the Tabernacle in all that specific detail – from the acacia wood, to the horns on the brass altar, to the placement of the cherubim.... We must become willing to have our inner temples reconstructed. The Bible says that we must be renewed in the spirit of our minds (Ephesians 4:23 KJV). It is the crucifixion of our limited ideas, the crucifixion of our fear, doubt, and worry. We must be crucified so we can rest; rest in God for the first time in our lives. Coming out of denial is the born-again moment.

In the Introduction I mentioned the book *Ancient and Modern Initiation* by Max Heindel (Heindel, 1986). Heindel interprets the opening lesson of the Tabernacle as this: "…the divine pattern of the path of progress is never given to anyone who has not first made a covenant with God that he will serve Him and is willing to offer up his heart's blood in a life of service **without self-seeking**" (emphasis mine). The initiate, who starts out "poor, naked and blind," must travel a long and grueling path before he can be illuminated and clothed in gorgeous robes before God and let God place that ring of union on his finger. First he must lay himself on the brazen altar and have the sin burnt from his flesh – again, the symbology of the sacrificial bulls and rams – and the stench rises from us and leaves us as we burn, as we willingly lay ourselves on the altar and say, "God, here I am. Make me whole. Make me complete. Make me sound of mind. Begin to work with me. I am willing to work with you." And thus the alchemical process can begin. Our common selves can be transmuted into holy oneness with the Father (just for the asking).

We remain free agents. We can live our entire lives in denial. God doesn't tell the alcoholic to stop drinking; the alcoholic must willingly surrender to God. We can live in fear, be angry, or stay addicted to pornography our whole lives until the end of days. But that's not what Jesus was talking about when he said "I have come that they may have life, and that they may have it more abundantly" (John 10:10). Jesus surrendered to the Father and opened to the Father and communed with the Father. He learned from what He suffered. We can do the same. We are invited to realize the Christhood that has always been there inside us, waiting only for us to ask.

You must find your own way out of denial. Have you ever tried to point out another person's problem to that person? "I see what's wrong with you," you might say. "You're fearful." You'd better get ready to put on the boxing gloves. And it's the same with the alcoholic or drug addict. Start talking to that alcoholic in denial about his drinking problem? He'll tell you he's not a drunk. There's some spiritual idea behind why he drinks. God made him this way. You can't push people into enlightenment. You can't take someone by the hand and yank them out of their stupidity or out of their fear, doubt, and worry. It's like the old Irish proverb Leland Kaiser likes to quote: "When the apple is ripe, it will fall." You need to let the apples ripen. People have to crash and burn. Like the story of the prodigal son, they have to hit bottom and start eating with the swine before they'll be ready to surrender. We are all prodigal sons. We have to come to the end of our "selves" and then surrender. And coming to the end of ourselves – stop and think about it – that's beautiful. The hope only breaks through when we understand that we're limited beings. But when we merge with an unlimited God, infinite things can happen and we will do the greater things. Just like Mother Theresa, Nelson Mandela, or any of the other enlightened ones in the world about whom you've read. God reached in and touched their spirits when they opened up and allowed Spirit into that deep place. Full surrender – fully surrendered space is the first step on the path through the Tabernacle.

Jesus' invitation was for us to walk in the same awareness toward the same enlightenment that He achieved. We can be whole and complete and know God loves us and wants to make us whole and complete. We have such a beautiful opportunity. We have the chance to walk in wholeness, to bring light into the world – real light – and to touch the hand of God. God will touch your hand, touch your heart, and touch your whole life. You will be made new. As we look at the Tabernacle gate, which also has been characterized as the kabala tree (the Tree of Life) we can see a working through our chakra systems and through the different elements of our bodies and minds. By *chakras* I refer to the energy centers in our bodies through which spiritual energy may flow. The seven chakras, as delineated by Hatha Yoga and other Eastern philosophies, are represented in the diagram.

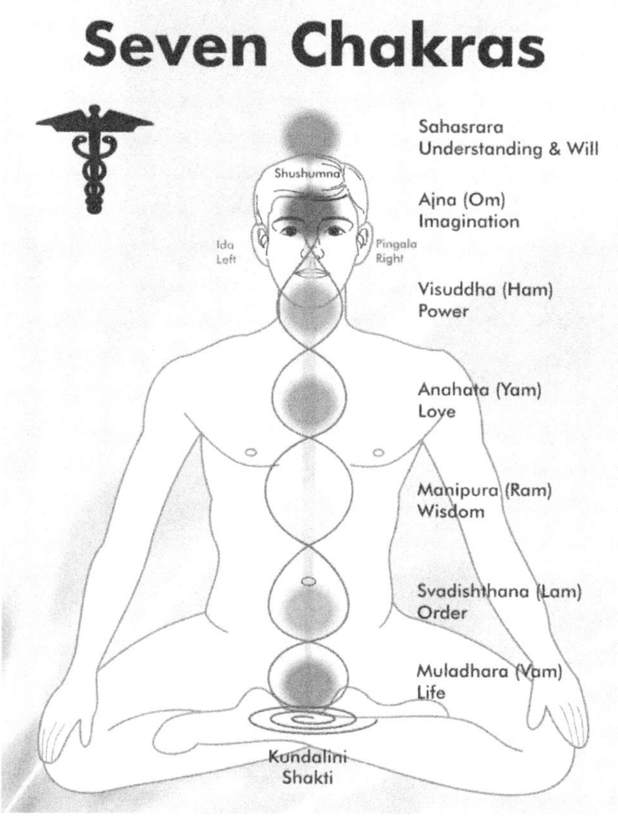

In the Tabernacle there will be a cleansing of our temples. Once we have lain ourselves on the brazen altar and surrendered, asked to be reborn, we next must become cleansed and purified. The glass must be polished so the light can shine through. The next chapter is about this cleansing process – bathing in the Bronze Laver. Your temple will be cleaned in your next stop along the path of learning, understanding, and making truth your own. Your path toward union with God.

CHAPTER 4:

BATHING IN THE BRONZE LAVER

I wish to be washed clean of my old life. To let go of my tide of sorrows and find my way to a new shore. ~William Joyce, *The Sandman and the War of Dreams*

The mind sees the world as a thing apart,
And the soul makes the world at one with itself.
A mirror scratched reflects no image—
And this is the silence of wisdom.
~Edgar Lee Masters

Nowadays people, especially Americans, seem obsessed with cleanliness. Spend five minutes watching daytime TV and we're almost guaranteed to see a commercial for "antibacterial" this or "germ-fighting" that. Or just type "cleanse" into the Google search box – that will call up hundreds of links to the latest detox or body cleanse craze.

I think perhaps this obsession with making our bodies (and abodes) clean stems from our deep inherent desire to connect with God. We've all heard the old proverb "cleanliness is next to godliness" and many people even believe that statement comes from Scripture. In fact no one knows the exact origin of the proverb, it does not appear in the Bible; and I believe the notion that being clean brings one closer to God is rooted in the symbolism of the Bronze Laver in the Tabernacle.

The Bronze Laver

Let's revisit the diagram I shared in the introduction: just inside the Tabernacle entrance stands the Altar of Burnt Offerings. This is the place where we, as initiates on the journey toward divine alchemy, have lain down and surrendered to a greater power. We've given up our "selves." We laid ourselves on the altar and said, "I give myself to God. God, help me." Each step along the pathway has such importance and no step can be skipped. This initial surrender is essential to open up our souls so the Holy Spirit, the spiritual dimension, can enter and merge with us. The next step along the pathway is equally important to surrendering on the Altar: we must bathe in the Bronze Laver.

"Then the Lord spoke to Moses, saying: 'You also shall make a laver of bronze, with its base also of bronze, for washing. You shall put it between the tabernacle of meeting and the altar. And you shall put water in it…When they go into the tabernacle of meeting…they shall wash with water, lest they die'" (Exodus 30:17-20). As metaphor the Laver implies not only a cleansing of the body but a cleansing of the soul from all stains of impurity. No one who is not clean in both body and mind may meet the Father and enter into union with Him.

Why should we bathe in the Laver? Why is washing an important step along the initiate's path? The deep reason behind taking the steps of surrender and cleansing, the reason why we are initiating this journey toward ultimate reward – union with God – is that we have realized that we have faulty navigation systems. And our navigation system is our matrix. It is the internal belief structure that has led us into addiction, religiosity, poverty, fear, unhappiness, or abuse. We have come to recognize the defectiveness of our belief infrastructures, the faults in our hardwiring. That's why now, at this very moment in life, at this junction where we have begun to read this book and chosen to follow the initiate's path – we are willing to become vulnerable to the spiritual dimension. We become ready to allow spirit to overshadow our bodies and minds. We are willingly and gradually becoming vulnerable to God. We are coming before the great "I am." We are stepping before the Divine Physician and asking Him, "Examine me" (thereby opening to the presence of God in our prayer and meditation).

Right now we have been granted a chance to return to the Garden of Eden, the place within us where all truth resides. Before we can find such grand truths within ourselves, the other temple – our ego man-made false temple – must be reconstructed and sometimes even torn down completely and rebuilt. This is the navigation system that we've used up to this point which is made up of all of our beliefs, doubts, worries….everything that's created this matrix that we live out of. A purging, if you will, would be like "out with the old and in with the new." So in this process of washing in the laver (which is our spiritual baptism, prayer and meditation), we are saying yes and opening up to divine guidance. The cleansing process of our inner temples, which is our beliefs, can now begin being reconstruction by the Holy Spirit. We must invite or say yes to the Holy Spirit (washing in the laver) that begins to wash over our dysfunctional beliefs to make them true and correct. By washing in the laver, we are saying, "yes" to being re-written by the highest power – God. We are promised in the Bible that we can be made totally new in the forces actuating our mind. So to me, prayer and meditation (washing in the laver) is like having a genie in a bottle that begins working on our behalf – just for the asking. Sometimes, our minds are like a full book. The pages are full. We've made up our minds. And by thus doing, there is no room for any divine ideas. So by washing in the laver (our prayer and meditation) the Holy Spirit, many times, has to tear out pages from our book so that we can hear God's voice.

Jesus said, "...he who believes in Me, the works that I do he will do also, and greater works than these he will do...And I will pray the Father, and He will give you another Helper, that He may abide with you forever – the Spirit of truth, whom the world cannot receive, because it neither sees Him nor knows Him; but you know Him, for **He dwells with you and will be in you**" (John 14:12-17; emphasis mine). This decision we have made: we will go it alone no longer. And we will not be left alone. The spirit will never ignore or abandon us. For "I will not leave you orphans; I will come to you" (John 14:18); "I will not leave you nor forsake you" (Joshua 1:5); and again Jesus said, "I am with you always, even to the end of the age" (Matthew 28:20).

Let me give an example. I was a Jehovah's Witness for more than four decades. That means I let the Watchtower Society and the Kingdom Hall be my navigation system (my matrix) for 40 years. The Witness ideology ran my life. My world view from my religious teachings was very negative. Everyone outside the door of the Kingdom Hall was going to die very shortly in the Battle of Armageddon. Everyone who was not part of my religion was "bad association" and "part of Satan's world" and we were told not to associate with that world. I could not play sports, have birthdays, attend college, or celebrate Christmas or any other worldly holidays. I had to take jobs that allowed me to take weekends off so that we could pass out Watchtower Magazines on Saturday and Sunday. My whole family became very dysfunctional and disabled, mentally, emotionally and physically. My mom spent most of her life in and out of hospitals; my dad became very obese. We were all just waiting for the world to end so that Jehovah would rescue/save us and so that we could then be ushered into God's Paradise on earth. This for me was a 40-year wait and that entire time, we felt that it would be over any day. So you can see by this that my matrix within my mind was very dysfunctional and why my world wasn't working very well. I'd begun drinking too, which only added to my suffering. My religious indoctrination was dysfunctional at best which is what kept me in a state of quiet desperation. This was my world and I decided to give this world over to God for re-construction. If I wasn't going to die soon or be of benefit to this world in any way, this temple (matrix) would have to be reconstructed or brought down completely. But there came a moment when I hit rock bottom. I was stuck. I'd sunk into a deep dark pit with no way out. But indeed there was a way out: I let go. I let go of some of my infrastructure, the angry god Jehovah, my fear and doubt-based beliefs, the religiosity, the Kingdom Hall and everyone I knew. I put them behind me and surrendered my "self" for something greater. I cried out in my deepest despair, "GOD HELP ME!" Like the prodigal son, I was sick of eating with the pigs, so I cried out to my Father and began my journey back home. The crying out, we remember, "God Help Me!" is us laying ourselves on the Brazen Altar – it's our surrender where the Holy Spirit has its invitation to begin its work of getting us back home. The washing in the laver is represented by our prayer and meditation which will be our inner GPS to navigate us back home, since we've travelled a long way. As time went on and I continued to be in a state of surrender (openness to hearing God's voice and spending time in prayer and meditation), and I eventually experienced the death of the "self" or the "ego" – the inner temple which Jesus said, "I will tear down this temple and rebuild MY temple……" As I continued this process of being cleansed by the waters of the laver, I noticed that my fears, doubts, worry, and regrets, shame, and hopelessness began to die down and faith, hope, and courage began to replace them and become stronger in me. Suddenly I began to see the wayshore in front of me. Things started to happen. I met people who helped and taught me. Books came into my hands. I became aware of other churches, new schools of thought to explore.

Bathing in the Laver is a metaphor for the willingness to open up and let the Spirit enter. Cleansing is a symbol for being a willing vessel, making our internal temples ready and open, saying yes and then trusting that the Spirit *will* enter, merge with us and rewire our infrastructures. It takes courage and strength to invite inspection from the Divine Physician and say to Him, "Examine me. Something's wrong. Make me whole, make me complete. Make me fearless. Get me unstuck. Lead me into greater prosperity." But the waters in the Bronze Laver are gentle and we are ready to bathe. When we are sick of eating with the pigs we become so ready to surrender and wash away our matrices. At this point, our minds will put up less resistance than we expected.

The Tabernacle as metaphor means far more than an outward structure. Sure, the Tabernacle was actually built at one time; it was a real tent that existed in the physical world. But our current task is to rebuild that temple *within ourselves*. As Max Heindel says, "We must build the Tabernacle within our own hearts and consciousness. We must become both the Altar of sacrifice and the sacrificial animal lying upon it…Later we must learn to identify ourselves with the mystic Laver, and we must learn to wash therein in spirit" (Heindel, 1986). We're talking about communing with God, communing with the Holy Spirit, bathing and resting in the Holy Spirit. The initiate must bathe in the waters of life, the waters of truth, and the waters of clarity to make ready to meet the Father face-to-face. So picture this Bronze Laver, this massive beautiful glowing bathtub, and then imagine us throwing off our robes and sinking into that soft pure water to wash.

The Mirrors of Reflection

The Laver has another attribute that's deeply important: its base is encrusted with mirrors. "He made the laver of bronze and its base of bronze, from the bronze mirrors of the serving women who assembled at the door of the tabernacle of meeting" (Exodus 38:8). Our challenge is to look into the Laver's mirrors and honestly see ourselves with all our stains, blemishes, and impurities. Looking into the Laver takes great courage. How many of us are willing to see ourselves as we truly are? Just being able to look in the mirror in the first place is so difficult. But consider this. In the Bible, Joshua challenged the Israelites to "choose for yourselves this day whom you will serve" (Joshua 24:15). I am asking that question today. Will we serve our illusions, our egos, and our false selves? Or will we look into the Bronze Laver; see ourselves clearly reflected in its mirrors and come out of all our denial? Will we look and learn and cleanse ourselves so we may serve the Father? We must look. We have to leave our disillusionments behind and wash away our blemishes, which in the Laver we now see with absolute clarity.

When we think about it, the mirror is not our enemy. It's our friend. Let's say someone is walking around with a spot of dirt on his cheek or a pimple on her forehead. Isn't that good to know? Wouldn't it be better to know it's there than walk around with a spot on our face that everyone else – except us – can see? We have the privilege of bathing in the Holy Spirit of truth. The waters in the Bronze Laver lead to transformation and life. We get to bathe in those waters, reflect in that still pool, and purify our minds until they are as clean as polished glass. Resting, relaxing and bathing in the Laver is no longer a daunting task. It's wonderful. The waters are gentle.

The Spirit Knows

Dwell for a moment on the water's gentleness, that tenderness. Like Father Keating says, the waters are gentle as "a drop of dew descending on a blade of grass" (Keating, 2006). That's the tender, loving hand of Christ; that's the Jesus I know. That's the hand that says, "Come with me. I'll help you through this. I'll walk you out of this addiction. I'll pick you up and carry you out of this addiction." That's the spiritual dimension, loving and gentle.

The spiritual dimension knows us. It knows everything about us. It understands the state we're in and how we got there. It knows where our parents came from, our grandfathers and their grandfathers all the way back to Adam. It understands the addictions, phobias, fears, and limitations that were handed down through the generations. It understands things our minds could never perceive. It understands what happened to us before we were born; it knows whether we were unwanted babies in the womb. It understands everything.

So there need be no self-criticism or flagellation – we are not required to beat ourselves up in order to meet God. We needn't scrub our skin raw or scour our internal floors with antibacterial bleach. The Father requires no whipping of the back or self-prostration. He simply looks down and says, "Dear one, if you could only see what I see. If you could only see the pathways of your forefathers, where they've walked and where they've been and what they've overcome." Aren't you grateful for this spiritual dimension within us, around us, above and below us? There's a spiritual dimension that knows and understands us. Isn't that wonderful?

We are invited to bathe in still waters so the cobwebs in our temples may be cleared away. The light in our temple is always there, the Kingdom of God always dwells within us. But cobwebs build up as byproducts of our illusions, uncertainties, and distrusts and block the light from shining through. The Laver is there to cleanse us of our demons and the idols we've allowed ourselves to worship before God – the temptations and falsehoods of our trickster selves. When we surrender to the spiritual dimension and sink down into the waters, the cobwebs wash clear and the light of pure truth can flow through us at any time.

Are you Ready to Bathe?

Here's another important point to grasp. This bath we're taking is not a one-shot thing. We are invited to soak in the Laver regularly and at any time. Being willing to look at ourselves, surrender our illusions, and wash clean on a regular basis is like dying and being born again over and over. Die and be born. Die and be born again. We may come to the Laver and bathe anytime we need. The surrender, cleansing, death and rebirth form a continual process. Die to error and be born again into truth. Then as our temples are rebuilt piece by piece, we may follow the initiate's path to the ultimate stop – the Holy of Holies – and thereafter walk in union with the Father all day, every day.

Some may wonder whether they're ready to immerse themselves in these cleansing waters. Some of us – like me – are so ready to take the plunge. My earlier book, *Surrender: Your Key to the Kingdom Within*, explains that there came a time in my life when I was literally sitting around waiting to die. I'd bottomed out. I wanted to die because I was dying anyway. I could feel the cold finger of Death upon my shoulder. I was angry, depressed, frustrated, hopeless, and desperate. My spirit inside was shriveling. And when the spirit dies the body is sure to follow; Spirit is the real source of life energy. The Bible says, "See, I have set before you today life and good, death and evil… choose life that you may live. This piece of Scripture means that if we live by the flesh our spirits will die; "…therefore choose life, that both you and your descendants may live" (Deuteronomy 30:19). Bathe in the Laver and be reborn into the new life.

Some people sink in bit by bit and wash in the Laver for years. Others jump in headfirst. The latter are those who, like me, just want to jump in, swim and be instantly cleansed from every impurity defiling their interior dimensions. They're so tired…tired of religiosity, tired of not feeling connected with God. Last month I went to an Inner Child Journey where I heard so many people saying they felt like their hands didn't meet God's hand, they couldn't touch. That's because they perceived the spiritual dimension as outside of themselves. It was "Christ out there," or "God over there." No connection to their internal temples. Yet God is within us even now. We only have to have our temple walls cleansed and we will feel His light shining out of us from the inside.

For some people the journey will take longer. People can't map the pathway to divine alchemy on a Microsoft Project timeline. We can't put each step into a pillbox and dose it out at one year, five years, or ten years. It is a process and we will move as fast as we will. As fast as we are willing to let God work with our interior dimensions. What an honor and a privilege! To be in life now, to serve now, to walk in union with the Father now. To be healthful and whole now. To be prosperous now – each in our own way. That doesn't mean we'll always be loaded with money. It means prosperity of thought, prosperity of having enough to make it, enough to fulfill our own needs and to share with others. Being prosperous enough to bless one another.

Let the process be what it is. All we are asked to do is begin it and a certain magic happens. All the forces of life and God come to the fore. Our temples will be rebuilt in their own time and gradually new thoughts and ideas will be revealed.

Dealing with the Smorgasbord of Information

As we wash away our selves and cleanse our inner temples of fears and worries, little by little new information will present itself. And when we examine new information and try to gain fresh understanding, often we will be asked to step outside our comfort zones. The material that shows up in our lives is likely to challenge the perspectives we hung onto when we lived inside a matrix. Other religions and unfamiliar ideas will cross our paths. Our task is to remember that now we are being guided by the Holy Spirit. We've surrendered and opened up to Spirit; now we must trust where it leads us. And where the Holy Spirit will lead us, is into truth.

Our minds want to believe that truth will be found in a single place. We might hit on a certain religious organization, a book, a spiritual or metaphysical teaching, whatever – and our minds will want to say, "This is it. I've found it. I've found the truth." There are a lot of gatekeepers out there. There will be a lot of people and churches with one eye on us, wondering where we're going and whom we are misleading. We have to be okay with that. We must give up codependency with other people and ask God to guide us. Otherwise we'll end up right back in the same box we were stuck in before or another box just like it. Others will try to drag us into the limited lives they're leading and the same fears that run their matrices. It happens all the time. People love to share their limitations and hopelessness. We can see fear, doubt, and worry written all over their faces – and they'll want to pack us up in their boxes.

Just know that while the internal temple is being reconstructed there will be an information-gathering stage and the information that comes up will be *specific to each individual*. No one else can rebuild another person's temple. A smorgasbord of information will appear, and we can fill our plates from that smorgasbord with hands and taste buds that are guided by God.

God is infinite. He cannot be contained in a box. To rebuild the temple in a way that invites Him to fill it we can't simply reconstruct another box like the one we left. Don't jump from one cult right into another. There is no absolute truth to be found in a single religion – or book – or spiritual leader. Rather, there is truth here and there; we will pick it up piece by piece from the smorgasbord as we go. Continue to open up, continue to wash clean in the Laver and stay outside the box. Move away from the matrix. We can't let the world news and TV ideology control and leave us stagnant. Those are Satan's food: "You cannot drink the cup of the Lord and the cup of demons; you cannot partake of the Lord's table and of the table of demons" (1 Corinthians 10:21). Of which smorgasbord will we partake? From the earthly dimension which is fear, doubt, and worry – the food of Satan? Or from the hope, love, joy, peace, and all the fruits of the Spirit which lay upon God's table?

The smorgasbord of information may seem intimidating at first, but we can give birth and move into this Christ dimension within our temples and let the Holy Spirit unfold in us. It's amazing. All we have to do is pray some for the journey, ask the Holy Spirit to overshadow us, and be patient with the Spirit and with ourselves as our old temples are dismantled and new ones are rebuilt.

Just Bathe in the Laver

So for now let go of the matrix. Step into the Laver. Rest in this bath, wash and bathe and relax. Say, "Lord, wash me clean. You're the one who can do this. You know me from east to west, from top to bottom. You know every hair on my head. You know every hair on my ancestors' heads. You know what's been passed down to me and what I'm dealing with, Lord. You know I want to, but for whatever reason, I'm incapable. So I surrender to Thee, Oh Lord." Subject yourself to the Holy Spirit and angelic direction will set a pathway. God will send messengers and a wayshore and a pathway out of the matrix. That's what we surrender into, what we are forming partnership with. The spiritual dimension will lightly and gracefully take us by the hand and lead. That's what we're merging with. That's the Laver – that's the gentle reflection the power works within us. That's the beauty of a loving God who gives everything back when we surrender and subject ourselves to Him. That's a step down the pathway toward the Holy of Holies which is meeting God face-to-face.

We can be part of all that. Just bathe in the Laver now.

CHAPTER 5:

THE TABLE OF SHOWBREAD

Baking bread is a lot like growing your faith in the Lord...You mix together the best ingredients you can find and wait for the mixture to mature, but it's the heat of the oven that makes it something of worth and substance. The same way the tribulations of this world mature a person's faith.
~Dorothy Love

If thou tastest a crust of bread, thou tastest all the stars and all the heavens.
~Robert Browning

As you have come this far on your journey, I hope it is becoming clearer and clearer that the Tabernacle I'm describing is not a literal building but rather a symbol for your own body and the temple of the Father being constructed within you. Remember what Jesus said? "'The kingdom of God does not come with observation; nor will they say, "See here!" or "See there!" For indeed, **the kingdom of God is within you**'" (Luke 17:20-21, emphasis mine). The kingdom of God is inside your body and your head. When you look beyond the literal meanings of Scripture you begin to comprehend that the whole Bible is allegory; it is written in a sort of code.

Let's review. First you entered the outer court of the Tabernacle sanctuary. You lay yourself on the Brazen Altar for sacrifice and surrendered to a power greater than your own. Then you bathed in the Bronze Laver and let yourself be washed clean of imperfections – broke out of the matrices that had enclosed you, your limitations and faulty hardwiring. You looked in the Laver's mirrors, saw your doubts and fears and worries in all their filth and ugliness and allowed them to be washed away. You became willing to be changed. You opened up and allowed Spirit to make you ready to enter the Holy Place.

Now as you enter the first Holy chamber – the second of the Tabernacle's three parts – your next stop will be to take communion at the Table of Showbread, which will be laid out on your right-hand side.

In Leviticus 24:5-8 the Lord spoke to Moses, saying: "'And you shall take fine flour and bake twelve cakes with it. Two-tenths of an ephah shall be in each cake. You shall set them in two rows, six in a row, on the pure gold table before the Lord. And you shall put pure frankincense on each row, that it may be on the bread for a memorial, an offering made by fire to the Lord. Every Sabbath he shall set it in order before the Lord continually, being taken from the children of Israel by an everlasting covenant.'"

According to these instructions, on the golden table before you reach the door to the Holy of Holies is "spread a blue cloth" (Numbers 4:7) upon which these twelve loaves are placed. And every week on the Sabbath the Israelites were to bake a new set of loaves. They were told to stand on either side of the table and, as priests on one side of the table removed the old loaves, those on the opposite side were sliding the new loaves into place; thus the showbread (literally translated, "bread of the face") was continually in the Lord's sight. These twelve loaves were placed atop each other in two rows of six. The loaves were huge: each single cake was made from two omers of wheat, and an omer is about five pints. It took ten pints of wheat to bake a single loaf? Those are gigantic loaves. And the bread was made from the finest wheat flour which was sifted through eleven separate sieves; oil, water, wine, and salt were the other ingredients. It was baked in special pans, painstakingly so as all the loaves would match perfectly in size and color.

Okay, that's the literal description of the showbread in the Tabernacle's second chamber. But what deeper knowledge and guidance can we glean from a metaphoric interpretation? In a recent article Hope of Israel Ministries have helped shed light on the mystery of the showbread (Keyser, 2014). First, the bread rests on a golden table; and gold represents the golden nature of God. Of the metals used in constructing the Tabernacle, this article explains, gold represents the Father; silver represents Jesus, the Son; and bronze represents man (us). Also are the loaves of bread golden, symbolizing our own spiritual transformation through divine alchemy. We are taking something simple (the flour, oil, salt, and water which stand for our lower selves, our base nature) and transforming it into something magnificent (golden bread, or God's nature rising up within us; our impending communion with the Father).

The showbread was prepared meticulously from the finest ingredients. Why was the flour sifted eleven times? That is us becoming purified. Sifting the flour through eleven separate sieves is just like us washing in the Laver to let all our blemishes and imperfections be eliminated. We must allow ourselves to become purified and prepared before we stand before the Lord.

The twelve loaves have been said to represent the twelve tribes of Israel. As it reads in Leviticus 24:8, the twelve cakes are "taken from the children of Israel by an everlasting covenant"; but who is Israel? Does that mean the showbread only has meaning for Jews? No. Look at what the apostle Paul had to say: "'For he is not a Jew who is one outwardly, nor is circumcision that which is outward in the flesh; but he is a Jew who is one inwardly; and circumcision is that of the heart, in the Spirit, not in the letter; whose praise is not from men but from God'" (Romans 2:28-29). The children of Israel are one big family, comprised not just of Jews but of all those who – like us – have surrendered their lives to God. The purification, the sifting has taken place and in special ovens our spirits have been transformed. We have been circumcised in our hearts and in the Spirit. Now we may offer ourselves to the Father as the showbread – purified, perfected, beautiful, luxurious loaves of golden bread.

The World Needs this Bread

I think the showbread in front of the Holy of Holies represents a communing. The people of Israel, that one family under God, have committed themselves to traveling this path; they have been circumcised from the heart and surrendered all their matrices and everything that's been holding them back. They've given their lives to God wholly and completely. Now they can enter into a constant covenant fulfilling the promise that they can commune with the Father whenever they will. That covenant is symbolized by the loaves of bread presented in front of God where He sits in the Holy of Holies.

This is what we become: this holy bread, pure and golden. And now we have answers. We have guidance. The way is pointed out for us. We realize the covenant that promises continual dialogue with the Holy Spirit. It's beautiful. When we need answers, answers appear. And we have answers for others. When we're talking with people and they pose spiritual questions, our purified selves will speak *for* and *through* and *as* us. Many times I've answered someone who asked me a difficult question and thought, "Who was that speaking? That wasn't me. That was such a brilliant thing to say, so perfect and true in this moment." The Holy Spirit speaks through us. The showbread – those huge golden loaves – was brilliant, lavish bread. We also become brilliant and lavish as we're transformed through divine alchemy into an individual representation of God, each of us in his or her unique way.

You surely know the words of the Lord's Prayer which appears in several Scriptural passages and includes the words: "Give us this day our daily bread" (i.e. Matthew 6:11). Just as we need to eat each day, to consume the bread of life, the world needs us to become this luxuriant golden bread. The world needs nothing less than our purified, perfected selves. The world needs the real us, the whole us, the divine us, the fully illumined man (or woman) of God to show up in all of us. Our opportunity at the Table of Showbread is to show up illumined with divinity and be representatives of God to one another. And along with becoming God's bread we will bring the joy, love, peace, wholeness, and completeness to the world – all those things the world so desperately needs.

Just Like Jesus

When our flour is sifted and our purified selves are baked into perfect golden loaves of showbread we become like Jesus. Jesus in fact called Himself "the bread of life" (see John 6:35, John 6:51) and this is the source from which the rite of communion was derived. "And he took bread, gave thanks and broke it, and gave it to them, saying, 'This is my body which is given for you; do this in remembrance of Me'" (Luke 22:19). Communion with God: transforming into a fully illumined person, a light of the world. That's exactly what Jesus was and Jesus called us into the same condition. We are called to become like Jesus, sons and daughters of God and lights of the world. We are to let our lights shine forth, not put them under a basket. We are to form a channel, a vehicle, a bridge so that Holy Spirit can touch the world through us.

This is the greatest expression of humanity on earth, to be fully alive with God in us – where *we* become less by being sifted and baked and allowing God's Holy Spirit to become *more* within us. Just to have the privilege to be the voice of God is unbelievable. To touch someone's life, to bring salvation to others through the Word, to let God's words pour out of our mouths is the single most beautiful opportunity we can grasp. Like Jesus we can save souls, uplift spirits, open the eyes of the blind into awareness; we can perform miracles. We can bring the dead back to life – that is, we can set others free out of that deathlike desperate state from which we were released when we started this journey. Like Jesus, speaking with the Father's voice and doing His will becomes our food. It is our bread of life.

What an opportunity! And this opportunity is for everyone, male and female, regardless of age or race or background or past religious affiliation. Now we have the grand opportunity to see God's kingdom from within. We can reach the high places within ourselves; awaken the forces that have lain dormant and illumine them with radiant light that comes directly from the Father. At the moment when you become the golden showbread and stand before the Father, you will go from glory into greater glory. You will begin to see as God sees and speak with His voice. You will speak with many tongues; you will know the tongue of understanding, the tongue that can reach another person's soul. You are getting closer to becoming one with the Father forever.

Being purified and baked into golden loaves is part of the process of rebuilding your temple and transmuting your soul into light. That light which is released to shine from within your temple out into the world around you is symbolized by the seven-branched candlestick in the Tabernacle, the next stop on your journey – described in the next chapter.

CHAPTER 6:

THE GOLDEN LAMPSTAND

Light must come from inside. You cannot ask the darkness to leave; you must turn on the light.
~Sogyal Rinpoche

I wish I could show you, when you are lonely or in darkness, the astonishing light of your own being.
~Hafiz

Several elements are essential to sustain human life as we know it. Clean air to breathe, clean water to drink, proper nutrients, movement, and basic health care build the foundation for our physical well-being. Healthy relationships, creativity, social support, service to community, and spiritual practice help us maintain mental and psychological health. But without one key element none of these other components could even exist. What is that most fundamental and vital element? Light.

Without the light of the sun our planet would freeze; photosynthesis would be impossible and all plant life would cease to exist; and without plant life neither humans nor any other animals could survive, as all the realms of nature are interdependent – woven together into the connecting fabric that sustains life on Earth.

Intuitively we all seem to understand how essential light is to our survival. But beyond simple physical necessity, we humans also have attributed light with a deep, powerful symbolism: it can stand variously for life, understanding, meaning, thought, creativity, goodness, love, beauty, and spiritual truth. In cartoons we represent the brainstorm of an idea by drawing a light bulb above a person's head. And in spiritual publications, how often have you seen a photograph of the sun's rays breaking through clouds to stand for God's presence?

Light is a good metaphor for God because God *is* light. In the last chapter we spoke about realizing your purpose, and now is a good moment to revisit the promise made to you on the first page of this book: you have been invited into union with the Father. And becoming one with the Father means you will be filled with His light. That's why the Bible resounds with light references: "Your word is a lamp to my feet And a light to my path" (Psalm 119:105). "Let your light so shine before men, that they may see your good works and glorify your Father in heaven" (Matthew 5:16). "There shall be no night there: They need no lamp nor light of the sun, for the Lord God gives them light. And they shall reign forever and ever" (Revelation 22:5). "For you were once darkness, but now you are light in the Lord. Walk as children of light" (Ephesians 5:8). "For it is the God who commanded light to shine out of darkness, who has shone in our hearts to give the light of the knowledge of the glory of God in the face of Jesus Christ" (2 Corinthians 4:6). And perhaps most important, "You are the light of the world" (Matthew 5:14). You will become the light just as Jesus promised. In one-ness with the Father you will become a light worker. You will bring light to the world.

Your face-to-face meeting with God is progressively approaching as you continue your journey deeper into the Tabernacle.

When you parted the veil and walked into the East Room of the temple, the Christ was lifted up in you just that much more; and as the veil was drawn aside you could see the altar of incense and the table of showbread quite clearly. But how could you see? Shouldn't it have been dark as you walked out of the sunlight and into this dim inner chamber? No, for on your left appears the Golden Lampstand upon which seven brightly-lit candles are set to illuminate your way.

The Seven Candlesticks

Just as the skies glow with light when the moon reaches its full phase in the east, so the East Room in the temple is filled with light; and that light is a visible symbol of God. The flames of the Golden Lampstand's candles are fueled by olive oil and thus have neither smoke nor odor; the sole purpose of their clear light is to dispel darkness. The candlelight indicates that you are coming nearer to His presence. For "God is the Lord, And He has given us light" (Psalm 118:27). By the same token, as you have surrendered and entreated the spiritual dimension to merge with your consciousness the light shining through your interior temple is growing stronger. "Arise, shine; For your light has come! And the glory of the Lord is risen upon you" (Isaiah 60:1).

It is no coincidence that the candles are seven in number: seven candlesticks may represent God's seven archangels – also called the Star Angels: "The mystery of the seven stars which you saw in My right hand, and the seven golden lampstands: The seven stars are the angels of the seven churches, and the seven lampstands which you saw are the seven churches" (Revelation 1:20). Seven often has been called a magic number. In 1956 psychologist George Miller coined "Miller's Law," which states that seven is the maximum number of chunks of information the human brain is capable of processing at once (Miller,

1956). Along similar lines, in a February 2013 blog post Joshua Tilghman relates the Tabernacle in the Wilderness to the human brain (Tilghman, 2013). Tilghman describes the seven candles as representative of the seven chakras, and the candlelight as metaphor for the kundalini energy flowing through the chakras: "Chakras help regulate conscious energy to all of our bodies. They resemble spinning wheels of light which act as gatekeepers for cosmic energy. When a person is spiritually ready and the chakras are open, kundalini has a chance to flow unobstructed to the brain where a conscious transformation takes place in the nervous system and endocrine glands" (Tilghman, 2013). Likewise our chakras must be illumined/opened before the Holy Spirit can enter fully. Surrender and patience are the keys to opening the chakras.

As the chakras open, they produce light that triggers the pineal gland; which in turn activates a higher level of consciousness. This elevated consciousness is the light of Christ being birthed in us. Note: This was the same Christ that was lifted up in Jesus. This Christ we're talking about here is not Jesus' last name. The Bible says that Jesus "became" the Christ or the Anointed of God. The Bible says that when Jesus died His passing ripped apart the veil in the temple: "And Jesus cried out with a loud voice, and breathed His last. Then the veil of the temple was torn in two from top to bottom" (Mark 15:37-38). The Christ (our new spiritual anointing) is being lifted up in us just as the veil between the inner sanctuary and the Holy of Holies was torn, allowing the light to flow forth from the place where we will soon meet God face-to-face – as Jesus reunited with the Father upon His death. Note: This death spoken of here is the death of the old man (Adam) and the raising up/birth of the new man – Christ, in you. Just as Paul said, "Christ in you, the Hope of Glory" (Colossians 1:27).And all this is happening within you. Your interior candles are being lit and the Christ is being born inside you as you welcome the spiritual dimension into your internal temple. You are being filled with light, the light of the seven candles which is designed to dispel darkness.

Bringing Light out of Darkness

So many humans today live in darkness. As I have shared before, I existed for many years with that inner dark – sadness, disillusionment with my religion, narrow-mindedness, hopeless desperation nearly to the point of suicide. During that time I knew virtually no light. So when I finally cried out for help and had my surrendered moment, I know that moment marked the beginning of my interior Christ being born. Light was shed and pathways opened up for me to walk. New pathways, new ideas, new religious and spiritual understanding was revealed by my freshly-kindled light/Christ in me. New people crossed my path to teach and help me, new books and literature came into my hands.

Here's another example from the Bible. Remember the apostle Paul? He is accredited with writing much of the New Testament. But prior to being recognized as Paul he was known as Saul. Saul was a Pharisee and a well-respected religious teacher. Immediately after Jesus' crucifixion and resurrection the Christ-followers began rising up and forming churches. But the new Christians were horribly persecuted, and Saul became a leader in the crusade to hunt Christians down and drag them to Jerusalem for execution. One day Saul was on his way to Damascus to arrest more Christians when a flash of light blinded him: "…suddenly a light shone around him from heaven. Then he fell to the ground, and heard a voice saying to him, 'Saul, Saul, why are you persecuting Me?' And he said, 'Who are You, Lord?' Then the Lord said, 'I am Jesus, whom you are persecuting'" (Acts 9:3-6). In that moment – with that blinding flash of light – Saul was changed forever. He was instantly converted; and from that day forward he was known as Paul the apostle. The Christ/the Anointing of God was downloaded instantly right there on the road, and Saul (now Paul) was changed forever. This was the virgin birth that could only happen by God's own hand (an immaculate conception). Paul's old self (way of being) was struck with blindness and then immediately after – he was given new sight, and the Light of Christ was born anew in him. And from that time forward, everything changed; the way he saw people. He now saw people the way God saw people. Similarly, if I had stayed in the dim light of Jehovah's Witness ideology, believing that we had the only truth and that everyone else on planet earth had it wrong, then I would be no different than Paul before his conversion into Christ awareness. Note: This would be my old man, my matrix, the part of me that is limited, lacking the full light of understanding that must die in order for a new awareness/new life, the new life of Christ, to be born in me. When we're stuck in a single idea and that's it, we've effectively closed out God, which means shutting out the light. As Wayne Dyer likes to say, the ego (E-G-O) edges God out (Dyer, 2011), and we live in complete darkness. To break free from ego rule and its narrow view of God, an illumination must take place.

We spoke earlier of the Scripture that reads (in the original King James translation), "The light of the body is the eye. If therefore thine eye be single, thy whole body shall be full of light" (Matthew 6:22). To me this passage describes what happens when the spiritual dimension (God) merges with our flesh, (the eye, or the "I," becomes single; that is, unified with God): you are filled with illumination (the whole body/human demeanor becomes bright). That's what is meant by the seven candlesticks on the Golden Lampstand. As those candles exist in your interior temple, God wants to light them. Through your experiential willingness to surrender and to say, "Yes, I want to be illumined," those candles will be lit by God's own hand. The spiritual dimension, the higher part of our selves, wants to be illumined and is drawn to the light. In this illumination His blessings will pour down upon you and lift you up. The Christos (the anointing of God) will rise up inside you. You will be anointed in your inner temple. A marriage will take place between your consciousness and the higher consciousness which is with God the Father. That opens the way for miracles. Real miracles are about to occur in your actual life.

Miracles

As I have traversed my own pathway through the Tabernacle, merged with the Holy Spirit and walked with the Father, I have continually been graced by miracles. These miracles manifest as downloads of information. Once I became able to paint beautiful pictures in a single day. My wife gave me an art set for Christmas. I'd never painted before and felt that I could not draw, let alone paint much more than a stick figure, but I decided to scratch some paint onto canvas just to make her happy. The next thing you know I had painted a gorgeous still life painting. That was a download from the Spirit. And I believe these information downloads are evidence of the interior illumination of the candlesticks, the inner light that God provides.

Like when I'm studying the Bible I will receive an insight and suddenly be able to understand with new clarity. One day I was reading about Jesus turning water into wine. From the Christian perspective that was a real and physical actuality. Ask any Christian and he'll say, "Yeah, the first miracle was Jesus turning water into wine." Okay, I thought, but the literal interpretation makes Jesus out as something of a hedonist (that is, a person devoted to the pursuit of pleasure), doesn't it? I mean, everyone around Him was feeling good already and here He was making vats of wine – hundreds of gallons of wine for these already feeling good people to consume. That seems rather hedonistic (pleasure-seeking) to me. But that's just the literal interpretation. The Bible has meaning far beyond the literal; much of the Book is allegory and symbology. Suddenly as I was reading I understood the Scripture about Jesus turning water into wine and various other passages in the Bible symbolically/ metaphysically, and esoterically.

Let's take a look at this story metaphysically for a moment. The wine represents Jesus Himself. Christ is the wine that never runs out. Man's wine, on the other hand, does run out; and man's wine is of fair quality at best. Think about the wine from the first part of your life. You start out and land your first job; you get married, buy a house, and have a baby. That's pretty good wine. It feels pretty good to have decent employment and move into that first home. But over time the linear things – that is, everything that happens in the outside world – start to deteriorate. Our bodies break down. Buildings crumble. Spiritual structures deteriorate too: maybe your pastor leaves your church and you lose that guidance and support. Man's wine runs out and goes bad over time. But the spirit – the wine of Christ – is constant and everlasting.

I wondered that day, "Why did I receive that awareness? Why was I reading about the wine in that particular moment?" And that's not the only time I've received such a flash of illumination. I received downloads about Moses going to the higher place, the mountain within himself to bring down the divine law; I was given clarity about the prodigal son story being symbolic of surrender at the Brazen Altar in the Tabernacle. These surges of understanding are the miracles that begin to occur from the moment we surrender and sacrifice our "selves," our egos, on the altar. That's when the magic starts and we begin to be filled with light. We are on a path to becoming the light of the world.

The Light of the World

When you surrender your ego on the altar and open your chakras, when you say, "I want to die to these narrow perceptions," you are overtaken by something greater, something more, and something vaster. There is a higher dimension of reality in which you can live. Ultimately that dimension is union with the Father. And the spiritual dimension is already there, within, in your interior temple; because Jesus said that this infrastructure, "the Kingdom of God is within you (us)." Jesus said, "I do not pray for these alone, but also for those who will believe in Me through their word; that they all may be one, as You, Father, are in Me, and I in You; that they also may be one in Us" (John 17:20-21). That is the coming into the Holy of Holies within your temple, walking with the Father and worshipping in spirit and truth. It means living life as a prayer. Your whole life becomes a prayer. You're here to serve; you're here to love your neighbors. That means all your neighbors, not just the ones who share your religion.

That is the meaning of the Golden Lampstand and the light from its seven candles. We want those candles lit; we want illumination. We want to walk in the light and be the light. When you walk in light, as Jesus said, "you are the light of the world." The light shines forth from within you to share with others you encounter. That's when you will experience greater things. "For the Father loves the Son, and shows Him all things that He Himself does; and He will show Him greater works than these, that you may marvel" (John 5:20). You literally will become a walking prayer. Your light will shine for others to see, for "No one, when he has lit a lamp, puts it in a secret place or under a basket, but on a lampstand, that those who come in may see the light" (Luke 11:33). As our walk becomes more and more illumined, it's natural that more blessings will flow due to the fact that Christ in us is changing us to become more like God and thus, in this sense, we go from glory to greater glory and experience more of God's divine giftings.

This is divine alchemy. This is spiritual alchemy: glory to greater glory. There can be no higher purpose than to surrender into this union and experientially receive the blessings which will appear in a pattern that is uniquely yours. The pathways the light reveals will make sense within your own framework of personal belief. My pathway will not be the same as the pathway of an Easterner who was born into Buddhism. A Christian's path will differ from the path of a Muslim. But we all are given that grandest hope – the hope of walking in union with the Father. The veil will be ripped in two. You and the Father will be one and you will be the light of the world.

CHAPTER 7:

HOLY GROUND:
Union with the Father

Once again, we are reminded that awakening, or enlightenment is not the property of Buddhism, any more than Truth is the property of Christianity. Neither the Buddha nor the Christ belongs exclusively to the communities that were founded in their names. They belong to all people of goodwill, all who are attentive to the secret which lives in the depths of their breath and their consciousness.
~Jean-Yves Leloup

Through life, I want to walk gently. I want to treat all of life – the earth and its people – with reverence. I want to remove my shoes in the presence of holy ground. As much as possible, I want to walk in peace.
~Steve Goodier

You have been treading the path of Moses as he built the Tabernacle in the Wilderness and set up all its accoutrements according to God's instructions. By now you know that all the Scriptural representations describing the Tabernacle were not only literally true during Moses' time but also may be used symbolically and esoterically to represent our present day. This temple – as you also should know by now – is being built within us by God's Holy Spirit. For example, read I Corinthians 3:16: "Do you not know that you are the temple of God and that the Spirit of God dwells in you?" and II Corinthians 6:16: "For you are the temple of the living God. As God has said: 'I will dwell in them and walk among them.'"

So now we stand at the grand climax of this symbolic Tabernacle in the Wilderness. This is where we meet God face-to-face, where we symbolically become His clear channel for expression for ourselves and for the world. This is the place in our lives where miracles will happen – instantaneously and often. Synchronicities will appear where we feel like we're "in the flow." We will experience great overwhelming feelings and expressions of love for our neighbors and friends. We have a great realization of this union with God. It's the same awareness to which Jesus wanted us to come when he said, "… that they all may be one, as You, Father, are in Me, and I in You; that they" [you and me!] "also may be one in Us" (John 17:21). It becomes our greatest desire to serve our neighbors. As Jesus said, it becomes our food to do the Father's will.

At this juncture it is interesting to read what the Rosicrucians had to say about the Shekinah glory as manifested in the Holy of Holies:

> **The Western Room of the Tabernacle was as dark as the heavens are at the time when the lesser light, the moon, is in the western portion of sky at eventide with the sun; that is to say, at the new moon, which begins a new cycle in a new sign of the zodiac. In the westernmost part of this darkened sanctuary stood the Ark of the Covenant, with the Cherubim hovering above, and also the fiery Shekinah Glory, out of which the Father of Light communed with His worshipers, but which to the**

physical vision was invisible and therefore dark.

We do not usually realize that the whole world is afire, that fire is in the water, that it burns continually in plant, animal, and man; yes, there is nothing in the work that is not ensouled by fire. The reason why we do not perceive this more clearly is that we cannot dissociate fire and flame. But as a matter of fact, FIRE bears the same relation to FLAME as SPIRIT to the BODY; it is the unseen but potent power of manifestation. In other words, the true fire is dark, invisible to the physical sight. IT IS ONLY CLOTHED IN FLAME WHEN CONSUMING PHYSICAL MATTER. Consider, for illustration, how fire leaps out of the flint when struck, and how a gas flame has the darkened core beneath the light-giving portion; also how a wire may carry electricity and be perfectly cold, yet it will emit a flame under certain conditions.

At this point it may be expedient to mark the difference between the Tabernacle in the Wilderness, Solomon's Temple, and the later Temple built by Herod. There is a very vital difference. Both the MIRACULOUSLY ENKINDLED FIRE on the Brazen Altar in the eastern part of the Tabernacle and the invisible SHEKINAH GLORY in the distant western part of the sanctuary were also present in Solomon's Temple. These were thus sanctuaries in a sense not equaled by the Temple built by Herod. The latter was, nevertheless, in a sense the most glorious of the three, for IT WAS GRACED BY THE BODILY PRESENCE OF OUR LORD, CHRIST JESUS, IN WHOM DWELT THE GODHEAD. Christ made the first self-sacrifice, thereby abrogating the sacrifice of animals, and finally at the consummation of His work in the visible world RENT

> **THE VEIL and opened a way into the Holy of Holies, not only for the favored few, the priests and Levites, but that WHOSOEVER WILL may come and serve the Deity whom we know as our Father. Having fulfilled the law and the prophets Christ has done away with the OUTWARD sanctuary, and from henceforth the Altar of Burnt Offerings must be set up WITHIN the heart to atone for wrongdoing; the Golden Candlestick must be lighted WITHIN the heart to guide us upon our way, as the Christ WITHIN, the Shekinah Glory of the Father, must dwell WITHIN the sacred precincts of our own God Consciousness. (Heindel, 1986)**

Note that the Shekinah glory is not visible to the physical eye but that the light must be kindled from within; only within the mind and heart may the initiate meet God face-to-face. And note also that Jesus opened up this glory "not only for the favored few," but for "whosoever will" know the Father. That means you and me and all of us on earth.

Now that moment has come in your life. Your moment has arrived: the realization of the Divine promise to which you were invited on the very first pages of this book. Yet that invitation has always been there. It was extended to you at birth. And it is not I who invite you. Jesus the Christ opened the way and God has called you to meet Him face-to-face, to walk with Him as He walks with you intimately from this moment forward. It is time for us to awaken ever more completely, continually shedding our damaged egos – to break free of the matrix, surrender our limited selves, become filled with glorious light, and then walk into the chamber known as the Holy of Holies and answer the call.

Our process as initiates has been to allow God, the Holy Spirit, and the Christ to reconstruct our own unique temples within ourselves. Willingness on our part is all that is needed for Christ to be raised up in us. That is the Shekinah glory in the cloud; that is the elixir, the invisible unseen essence that is God sitting in the Mercy Seat. In Scripture the whole Tabernacle formed a receptacle in which God resided. That means our brains and bodies have been God's dwelling place forever, and will remain so…forever. In the Bible that final chamber, the Holy of Holies, was a special place where God's glory would manifest and which no priest (read: human being) could enter without meticulous preparation and cleansing. This preparation also was represented by the showbread which was prepared to perfection: it was made with the finest flour. The portions of dough were measured out exactly. The bread was sifted eleven times. That is the preparation we've been undertaking as we have continued our journey through our symbolic interior temple. We have lain ourselves on the altar. We have surrendered to Spirit (the "power greater than ourselves" in the Twelve Steps). We have been guided by the Holy Spirit to bathe in the Bronze Laver, which is the beginning of our spiritual baptism brought about by prayer and meditation. We have baked and eaten the showbread and become illumined by the candles on the Golden Lampstand. Now it's time to part the veil for the final task on this journey: push the veil aside and step into the Holy of Holies.

Let's take a moment to look at the actual mystical mechanics of this step. Metaphorically the Holy of Holies within your mind is represented by the left and right hemispheres of the brain becoming one. For most of us the left brain dominates our mind with that kind of "survival of the fittest" mentality acting on its own. As we become increasingly aware of our thinking capacities, we come into union with a new partner which is faith, hope, and love. Those qualities live in the etheric right side of our brain. This right brain hemisphere many times must be re-activated by our willingness to open up and receive help as we do when we say, "God, help me."

Many examples of the right brain can be found symbolically in Scripture and in the physical world. The sun rises in the east which is to the right as we read a map. The Bible tells us that when Solomon built his temple for the Lord, "The doorway for the middle story was **on the right side** of the temple" (1Kings 6:8; emphasis mine). And when Jesus came upon his disciples fishing He asked, "'Children, have you any food?' They answered Him, 'No.' And He said to them, 'Cast the net **on the right side** of the boat, and you will find some.' So they cast, and now they were not able to draw it in because of the multitude of fish" (John 21:5-6; emphasis mine). These are further allegories representing your right brain which is the spiritual dimension within you that must be activated.

As we begin to use this right hemisphere continuously, opening up to and surrendering to Holy Spirit, a cloud begins to form between the wings of the two cherubim located on the Ark of the Covenant (right and left brain). This is where the Most Holies is located – the Lord's cloud resides between the two parts of the brain, between the two cherubim. Within the Ark between the two wings, the two spheres of the brain, when right and left come together as one, there lies the glory of the Lord. That is the spiritual dimension within us; that is the Kingdom of God within in all its glorious array. As these two parts of our brain become fully activated and begin to work wonderfully in union, the eye becomes single (as Jesus said) and the whole body is bright. The "eye becoming single" represents the pineal gland, an endocrine gland of the human brain which sits right in the middle of the forehead. When these two brain hemispheres move into harmonious balance the spiritual energy can run up and down through the body temple, illuminating all the chakras rising up to the pineal gland (the Holiest of Holies) within our very minds (temples). And working in concert the two halves of our brains focus perception not dimly like a flashlight, but like a laser in brightness and clarity. *You have met God face-to-face.*

They Should Teach this in Church

We will continually meet God in various flashes of awareness and brilliance within the new understanding of our mind's temple. Just like Paul of Tarsus traveling on the road to Damascus saw the flash and had that sudden awareness of meeting Christ face-to-face. That mystical meeting changed Paul forever. And we too may have these mystical, prescient occurrences. Maybe we're able to stop smoking easily. Or we stop losing our temper. Or we overcome some obstacle that we previously found insurmountable. We finally find the power to ask our boss for that raise. We find our purpose. This too is like Paul: our Most Holy encounter with God is continual throughout the rest of our lives. Divine light shines from within. We are the Lord's vessels, His mouthpieces, and His conduit in ways now that we never dreamed possible.

There's a drastic need for the churches to help followers find this place within themselves and to say, "This is the good news of the Kingdom, the Kingdom of God is within you," instead of trying to serve as mediators between their congregations and God. But the churches have a dim view of this union at best. Few – if any – churches will teach us that we can be like Jesus and tap into the Kingdom within. And yet Jesus said, "'Most assuredly, I say to you, he who believes in Me, the works that I do, he will do also; and greater works than these he will do'" (John 14:12). The same Jesus who walked on water, cast out demons, healed the terminally ill – we can do the same works He did. Isn't that exciting?

Here it's important to note that "Christ" was not Jesus' last name. It was his title – Jesus *the* Christ. Christ means "anointed of God." Jesus the Anointed of God. And Jesus was calling all of us to become anointed and do the things He did. Jesus told us we have access to the same power He had. Jesus was inviting us into a grand marriage arrangement, Union with Him and with the Father here today…on earth…now. And the truth about this arrangement between us and the Father is the truth that sets us free.

Divine alchemy, union in the Most Holies is converting our lower self, the ego (dark dense matter, imperfect flesh) and transforming that false self into pure perfected gold.

How do we Know we've "Got It?"

How can we know when this perfect divine union is taking place within us? The biggest transformation that has happened to me is that there is no longer "me" versus "them." All judgment of others is gone. I can love the Buddhist, the Christian, the Muslim, the Hindu, and the atheist all the same. We may begin to have gifts show up related to our understanding of spiritual ideas. We finally have the strength to leave that dysfunctional relationship. We have more inner strength. Maybe we finally begin writing that book for some reason. Things usually begin to change from the mediocre to the great. Mentally and emotionally we are happier, more joyful about life, empowered instead of victimized and immobile.

Another transformation I experienced is that I suddenly became able to grasp the metaphysical, symbolic and esoteric meanings behind the literal Bible stories – the philosophy, the ties to Greek mythology. There are many levels of understanding within the Scriptures. We limit ourselves when we perceive only the literal interpretation of the Word, when the Bible actually has so many dimensions. Look at the story of Job. Read the book of Job literally and it says Satan met God in heaven and God told Satan there was no one on earth like Job. And at the beginning Job looked great. He had a home, plenty of food, a great family, and lots of livestock. In today's terms Job would've been the guy with the 3,000 square foot split-level with the pretty fence and the artful landscaping; a trophy wife, successful kids, and a couple of BMWs in the garage – in other words, he had all the goodies. So Satan wanted to tempt Job to prove that he would crack under pressure. And God said okay, Satan, give it a try. You can take everything Job has except his life.

So Satan took Job's belongings away, killed his children and his cattle, brought him to his knees and covered him with boils. Then he sent Job's three friends to counsel Job that his downfall was his own fault: he must have done something bad or this wouldn't have happened. When you read this only from the literal perspective you might wonder, "When will *my* test come? Just how far will God let Satan go to test me?" But when the Holy Spirit enables us to delve a little deeper into the symbology of this Scripture, we see that at a core level fear was running Job's life. "For the thing I greatly feared has come upon me. And what I dreaded has happened to me" (Job 3:25). Fear was Job's limitation, his matrix. Metaphorically that fear represents Satan and as we know when fear (limitation) runs our inner temple, destruction occurs. That's what happened to Job. But Job remained faithful throughout all the tests Satan posed for him and was finally rewarded with ten times what he had. Job overcame his fear and remembered that God was all good; God was the beginning and the end and there was nothing to fear. Then his reward was peace, prosperity, wholeness, everything he had before returned tenfold. It's the same for us. It's our inner dimension that we need to heal using the Spirit of Truth.

We all have those inward fears whether we know it or not. Fear that we're not going to get a job. Fear that we won't find a suitable mate. Fear that there's not enough money to pay our bills. Surrendering fear at the gate of the Tabernacle and laying that fear on the altar to be crucified (given up to God) is the answer. Let's go back to Job. Even after Satan (fear) had taken all his goodies away, Job still believed this wasn't the whole story. He still was able to say: "'I know that You can do everything. And that no purpose of Yours can be withheld from You…I have heard of You by the hearing of the ear, But now my eye sees You." [Wow, greater and greater understanding.] "Therefore I abhor myself, and repent in dust and ashes'" (Job 42:2-6). God gives Job back all he had and more. The Scripture reads, "And the Lord restored Job's losses when he prayed for his friends. Indeed the Lord gave Job ten times what he had before…Now the Lord blessed the latter days of Job more than his beginning; for he had fourteen thousand sheep, six thousand camels, one thousand yoke of oxen, and one thousand female donkeys. He also had seven sons and three daughters" (Job 42:10-12).

This is the awareness that comes when we overcome a limitation. That is the tenfold realization of opportunity that we experience when we break out of a matrix, and enter the divine kingdom within in all its magnificence.

Enlightenment is simply a fully expanded awareness of the infinite possibilities that God has provided. So there's no end to this meeting with the Father face-to-face. There's just an expanding love into infinitude within our minds, our temples. Jesus said that we – you and me – would be the light of the world. You and I would be one in union with the Father. It would be our food to do the Father's will. Great things we would do because the Father (Spirit) would be doing it with us. And what we speak also will be of the Spirit. Wow!

Your New Truth

As we continue walking this path and invoking the Holy Spirit of Truth within our temples, in time we find that the surrender, the dying to the lower nature (fears, pride, materialism, and excesses) and being born again, dying and being born again, letting go of the old and embracing the new divine awareness, washing in the laver, polishing the glass and cleansing our interior temples, allowing inner illumination with the golden light from within – all these actions will autonomously, automatically and with very little prompting continue to work on our inner selves to become better. As this cooperation between Holy Spirit and matter continues, we desire all veils to be removed from our eyes and all roadblocks taken from our paths. We want truth at all costs. We are willing at a moment's notice to replace any non-serving, limiting belief when a better one is presented. There is no ego (E-G-O, Edging God Out) to stop this veil from lifting; it's truth at any cost from this point forward. If someone presents a nugget of higher understanding, we can embrace it because it's better, it's more profound, and it's truer than what we previously believed. We can just grasp onto that new, shiny golden nugget and let the non-truth float away like dross, like fool's gold. An interior purification of absolute knowing begins to dominate our temple. The process becomes wonderful.

The Bible talks about the two becoming one, remember, "…if therefore thine eye be single, thy whole body shall be full of light" (Matthew 6:22, King James Bible version). Now the two sides of your brain are being sewn together, stitch by stitch; a marriage garment is taking form that weds the left side (ego) to the right (spiritual dimension) and the Holy Spirit rises up in the middle of the two hemispheres. You checked your denial at the gate. You retired your suffering. You've come to the end of yourself and said you were no longer willing to walk alone. "For indeed, the kingdom of God is within you" (Luke 17:21). Now you are in God's hands and God's hands are on you. Divine alchemy is occurring on all levels of your inner being.

Now that we are communing with the Spirit and Truth within us, union with the Father in the inner kingdom, we have granted God *carte blanche* to download information. And He will transfer downloads of profound wisdom and knowledge. Our confidence grows. As the knowingness that we're no longer alone solidifies, miracles start to happen. Prosperity will become easier. Opportunities for work and creativity will show up. Many things will happen in this union because we are now walking in a purer faith day by day. We see from new angles, think differently, and love differently. The spiritual gifts from God begin to saturate us. The Christos was born in us and it will take greater and greater dominion over our actions. The Holy Spirit will use our mind, our tongue, our hands and our body. We will be exactly what the Father needs us to be in that precise moment. We can be comfort, healing, eye-opening – all the things Jesus did and greater we will do.

Holy Ground

As we continue to walk the walk, the divine order of alchemy becomes more automatic. The Holy Spirit continually releases more and more of the truths that set us free. What a wonderful thing to meet God face-to-face in the Mercy Seat, the inner sanctuary of our mind changing us moment by moment. The great permeation of Spirit that rises up inside is the same Spirit that permeated Jesus. It's like a virus. It permeates, saturates, possesses. Spirit completely diminishes the lower self; it eats up our dysfunctional nature (ego). God called us to move into our higher selves and we become cleaner vessels through which He will shine light, music, beauty, and truth forevermore.

Then what happens is that we enter a rest. We enter a peace. We may not be perfect, but as we move into greater understanding of God's love and God's nature we begin to embody that nature which will radiate out for the benefit of others.

Once this spiritual impregnation has given birth in us we can go into any church with love. Love knows no boundaries. We can take our love into any part of the world. The Christ (God's love) can go anywhere. The Christ that dwells in us, the Spirit of God, the hope of glory, the awareness of the illumined space that lives inside our temples can light any place, in any country and inside any building and on any mountaintop and at the bottom of the ocean. The divine gold is who and what we are and we bring it with us wherever we go. Just like Jesus having a drink with the tax collector or eating supper next to the prostitute, we bring that golden light (love) to all whose lives we touch.

Then any spot where you stand becomes holy ground. Every moment in your life is a sacred moment. You have a deep, deep abiding soul connection with God. Every look you give another person; every word out of your mouth; every footstep you take is holy. We walk on ground that is holy because of our new keen awareness of this perfect moment. We have become a conduit to spread the Father's light and love to the world and working through us He sanctifies the very ground where we step.

This is our new reality, this constant oneness with the Father.

Daniel Clark

Everywhere we walk is holy ground.

CONCLUSION:

UNION IS FOREVER

As the Christ said, "I go to my Father," when He was about to be crucified, so also the Servant of the Cross who has made the most of his opportunities in the visible world is allowed to enter the glory of his Father Fire, the invisible Shekinah Glory. He ceases then to see through the dark glass of the body, and beholds his Father face to face in the invisible realms of nature.
~ Max Heindel, *Ancient and Modern Initiation*

You have reached the final chamber in your interior Tabernacle and met God face-to-face. Therefore this is the place where my book must end. But I don't want to leave you until I am sure you understand that stepping into the Holy of Holies and meeting God's glory on the Mercy Seat is not the end. The process of enlightenment of our interior temple is a continual process that goes on forever.

We will go back many times to revisit all the various chambers within our inner temple. Our temple is always under construction.

Eventually we enter what the Bible calls the rest. This rest, once again, is the peace, the tranquility, the trusting which grows in us as we become more and more holy. However, we must have eyes to gain the secret ancient understanding to see the pathway. Our eyes must be opened by God himself.

The spiritual dimension will continue to burst forth in you just like the flower that was meant to shine forth in all of its beauty. Soon there will be no greater work for you than to serve God, to serve your brothers and sisters, and be of service to the world. Doing the Father's will becomes your food. Your food, your life sustenance will be to show up in the world as love, joy, and peace.

Where you stand, God is. Where you walk, God walks; and that is holy ground. When you speak, truth is spoken through you. Wherever you go, church is. You have not become God. You have become God's house. He resides in you and He is the one who opens your mind to continual, ongoing, infinite possibility. As you continue to co-operate with the Holy Spirit, symbolically, you and the Father are as one.

Your boxes have been broken and you are set free. So you have relinquished the matrices and the titles that once defined you. Your awareness expands; it grows to infinite proportions. It becomes *uncontainable*.

Go forward in grace!

GLOSSARY

Alchemy: The process of taking something common and transforming it into something of great value.
Ark of the Covenant: A chest containing the stone tablets upon which the Ten Commandments were inscribed. The Ark resides in the Holy of Holies, the final chamber in the Tabernacle in the Wilderness.
Bronze Altar: An altar of sacrifice situated just inside the gate of the Tabernacle in the Wilderness. In this book, the altar symbolizes the first step on the journey toward Divine Alchemy – the place where initiates surrender their baser "selves" to God and allow Holy Spirit to enter.
Bronze Laver: A bronze basin which sat between the Bronze Altar and the first chamber in the Tabernacle in the Wilderness. For this book, the laver represents a place of cleansing, where the initiate washes away faulty belief systems to make ready for Holy Spirit to reside within.
Chakras: Energy centers in the human body through which spiritual (kundalini) energy flows. (See diagram in Chapter 3.)
Denial: A mental defense mechanism by which a person avoids facing a painful truth by refusing to acknowledge its existence.
Divine Alchemy: A spiritual pathway toward meeting God and becoming one with Him; transforming one's lower (base) self into pure spirit.
Golden Lampstand: A lampstand hammered from a single piece of gold into seven branches. The Lampstand was located opposite the Table of Showbread in the first chamber of the Tabernacle in the Wilderness. In this book the Lampstand symbolizes kundalini (chakra) energy, illumination from within by the Holy Spirit, and the birth of Christ within us.

Holy of Holies: The final chamber in the Tabernacle in the Wilderness, where the Divine Alchemy initiate metaphorically meets God face-to-face.

Kabala Tree: The Tree of Life; another metaphor for the Bronze Altar in the Tabernacle in the Wilderness, where the initiate surrenders the self to God.

Matrix: Any belief system which we allow to control our thoughts and actions.

Pineal Gland: A small endocrine gland in the human brain. For this book's purposes the pineal gland represents the opening of the Sahasrara (understanding) chakra to allow light to flow through, activating one's higher consciousness.

Shekinah Glory: The Divine Presence of God. In the Tabernacle in the Wilderness, God's Shekinah Glory settles or dwells in the Holy of Holies, in the Holy Seat before the Ark of the Covenant.

Showbread: An offering of twelve loaves of bread which were placed on a blue cloth on a golden table just outside the door to the Holy of Holies in the Tabernacle. In this book the showbread symbolizes a covenant between God and the initiate, whereby the initiate surrenders (offers) his or her life completely to God, and thus may experience union with God in every moment thereafter.

Tabernacle in the Wilderness: a portable temple built by the Israelites to worship God during their travels in the desert. God provided specific instructions as to how the Tabernacle should be built and adorned (see Exodus 25). For the purposes of this book, the Tabernacle is interpreted as allegorical, with each chamber and component of the temple symbolizing a step along the initiate's path toward Divine Alchemy.

BIBLIOGRAPHY

Debus, A.G., 2004. Alchemy and early modern chemistry: Papers from Ambix. Jeremy Mills Publishing.

Dyer, D.W.W., 2011. Excuses begone!: How to change lifelong, self-defeating thinking habits, 4th ed. Hay House, Carlsbad, CA.

Heindel, M., 1986. Ancient and modern initiation, 5th Edition. ed. The Rosicrucian Fellowship, Oceanside, CA.

Keating, F.T., 2006. The more subtle kinds of thoughts, in: Open Mind Open Heart: The Contemplative Dimension of the Gospel. Continuum International, London, UK.

Keyser, J.D. (Ed.), 2014. Mystery of Mysteries -- What is the Showbread?

Merriam-Webster, Inc., 2014. alchemy. Merriam-Webster.

Miller, G.A., 1956. The magical number seven, plus or minus two: Some limits on our capacity for processing information. Psychol. Rev. 63, 81–97. doi:10.1037/0033-295X.101.2.343

Reid, N., 2008. The spiritual alchemist: Working with the voice of your soul. River Daughter Press.

Robertson, R., 2009. Indra's Net: Alchemy and chaos theory as models for transformation. Quest Books, Wheaton, IL.

Tilghman, J., 2013. What the Twelve Tribes of Israel and the Tabernacle really symbolize. Spirit Scripture.com.

Made in the USA
Las Vegas, NV
12 June 2026

48611089R00056